DICTIONARY OF NAUTICAL ACRONYMS AND ABBREVIATIONS

DICTIONARY OF NAUTICAL ACRONYMS AND ABBREVIATIONS

Donald Launer

SHERIDAN HOUSE

First published 2006 by
Sheridan House Inc.
145 Palisade Street
Dobbs Ferry, NY 10522
www.sheridanhouse.com

Copyright © 2006 by Donald Launer

All rights reserved. No part of this publication may be reproduced, stored in a retrieval system or transmitted in any form or by any means, electronic, mechanical, photocopying, recording, or otherwise, without the prior permission in writing of Sheridan House.

Library of Congress Cataloging-in-Publication Data
Launer, Donald
    Dictionary of nautical acronymns and abbreviations / Donald Launer.
    p. cm.
  ISBN-10: 1-57409-239-1 (alk. paper)
  ISBN-13: 978-1-57409-239-4 (alk. paper)
    1. Naval art and science—Abbreviations—Dictionaries.
  2. Naval art and science—Acronyms—Dictionaries. I. Title.

V23.L38 2006
623.801'48—dc22　　　　　　　　　　　　　　　2006024398

ISBN 10: 1-57409-239-1
ISBN 13: 978-1-57409-239-4

Printed in the United States of America

Contents

Introduction
vii

PART I
Common Acronyms and Abbreviations
1

PART II
Excerpts of Abbreviations from NOAA's Chart No. 1
123

Introduction

I was reading a nautical technical journal and came across an abbreviation with which I was not familiar. Although I have had a USCG captain's license for twenty-five years, and I have written over 300 articles for recreational boating magazines, I was stumped. I have an extensive library of boating books, including dictionaries, glossaries, and technical treatises, but I found that there was no reference book where I could look up nautical abbreviations and acronyms. Obviously there is a need for such a reference work; one that translates the industry's and the government's abbreviations into plain English.

Today, abbreviations, acronyms, and truncations are being used with increasing frequency. This is partly due to the widespread use of more sophisticated equipment on board, along with their associated complexities, and partly due to the sometimes mistaken belief that these abbreviations simplify explanations and identifications.

For those new to boating, this problem is especially daunting, since it seems as if they are listening to, or reading, a foreign language. While many nautical terms in themselves can be confusing, some of the acronyms and abbreviations can be bewildering; and the many new abbreviations dealing with modern electronics can be mystifying, even for old salts.

So, for both the neophyte as well as the seasoned skipper, this book contains most of the definitions of abbreviations and acronyms that will be encountered in recreational boating.

PART I is an alphabetical listing of acronyms and abbreviations. Needless to say, not every acronym or abbreviation can be included. Most companies have their own lettered abbreviations for their names as well as for proprietary products and, for the most part (except for those I feel are of special value) these abbreviations have not been listed. I have used my own discretion in this respect. The military also uses some special abbreviations which will seldom be encountered by the recreational boater, and I have weeded out many of these along with some of the more esoteric abbreviations, as well as some so specialized that they will almost never be encountered.

It should also be noted that some of the abbreviations listed, those used on charts, are shown in italic type. This is pursuant to NOAA's protocol that hydrographic features—that is, those features below the high-water datum as well as floating objects—should be in italics on charts. Charts from other countries do not necessarily follow this rule.

PART II is an abridged version of a U.S. Government publication known as *Chart No. 1, United States of America: Nautical Chart Symbols, Abbreviations, and Terms*. This publication provides the symbols and abbreviations used on all U.S. charts, whether paper or electronic, as well as those nautical abbreviations used by the U.S. Coast Guard and other governmental agencies. Unfortunately, the *Chart*

Introduction

No. 1 booklet, once available from all NOAA chart dealers, is no longer in print from the Government Printing Office, which makes this section of the book even more valuable as a reference tool.

PART I

COMMON ACRONYMS AND ABBREVIATIONS

A

a   an abbreviation for *amperes*, the measurement of current flowing in an electrical circuit. An *ampere* is defined as the steady electric current produced by one volt applied across a resistance of one ohm. *See* Amps; mA

aband   an abbreviation used in NOAA charts to indicate *abandoned* (i.e. aband lt hs, would be an *abandoned light house*).

ABBRA   an acronym for the *American Boat Builders and Repairers Association*, which was founded in 1943 to serve, strengthen, and encourage workers in the marine service industry through a search for solutions to common problems and the sharing of knowledge.

ABS   an acronym for the thermoplastic polymer *acrolonitrile butadiene styrene*, which is used for the production of small boats as well as accessory items.

ABS   an abbreviation for the *American Bureau of Shipping*, which promotes the security of life, property and the environment through developing standards for the design, construction, and operation of marine-related facilities.

ABYC   the *American Boat and Yacht Council* is a non-profit membership organization that has been developing and updating the safety standards for boat building and repair for 50 years. It also provides certification programs for marine technicians. The membership of ABYC includes boat owners, boat builders, surveyors, boat yards, insurance companies, law firms, trade associations, marinas, dealerships, government agencies, and equipment and accessory manufacturers.

AC   an abbreviation for *alternating current*.

AC   an abbreviation for the *America's Cup*. See also ACC

ACC   an *America's Cup Class* boat is the class of boat used for the 32nd America's Cup. It is designed to a specific rule with several trade-offs in length, weight, and sail area, and must be built in the country of origin of the yacht club the team represents. The ACC has been used for America's Cup competition since 1992.

ACBS   the *Antique and Classic Boat Society* brings people with an interest in historic, antique, and classic boats together for the exchange of information, experience, and ideas. It serves as a communications channel in the preservation and restoration of classic boats.

ACCSP   the *Atlantic Coastal Cooperative Statistics Program* is a state/federal program that designs, implements, and conducts marine fisheries statistics data collection programs, and integrates those data into a single data management system that will meet the needs of managers, scientists, and fishermen.

ADF   an *automatic direction finder*. See RDF

ADFG the *Alaska Department of Fish and Game* division was established in 1951 as part of Alaska's territorial government to oversee Alaska's developing sport fisheries. The division is responsible for the overseeing and management of Alaska's sport and personal use fisheries.

af *audio frequency* or *audio frequencies* are those frequencies audible to the human ear and are approximately between 15 Hz and 20 kHz. *See* Hz

AFRAS in 1976 a group of professional seamen and business men established the *Association for Rescue at Sea, Inc.*, a non-profit foundation that supports services concerned with saving lives at sea.

AGM an *absorbed glass mat* storage battery features dense glass mat separators, compressed and joined into the battery's plates, reinforcing these plates. AGM batteries have better starting power, shock resistance, and deep-cycle capabilities than most other types of storage batteries.

Airsta the Coast Guard's abbreviation for *Coast Guard Air Station*.

AIS the Coast Guard's *Automatic Identification System* operates on VHF channels 87B and 88B, and is currently only mandatory for large, commercial vessels. When interfaced with a GPS/chart plotter and/or radar display, it picks up signals from other AIS-equipped vessels within VHF range and indicates their positions on the screen, with the vessel's name, call sign, heading, speed, and MMSI number. Because of the current high cost of AIS equipment, as well as some technical considerations, there are no immediate plans to make

AIS mandatory for recreational craft; however newer, lower-priced AIS equipment may change this policy for larger, offshore, recreational vessels. See MMSI

AIWA　the *Atlantic Intracoastal Waterway Association*'s mission is to encourage and further develop waterborne commerce and recreation in the intracoastal waterways of Virginia, North Carolina, South Carolina, Georgia, and Florida through the promotion of adequate dredging, safe navigation, and maintenance.

al or **alt**　an abbreviation used in NOAA charts to indicate *altitude*.

A.M.　*amplitude modulation* is the modulation, or change, in the amplitude of a radio wave in accordance with the strength of an audio or other signal that conveys information.

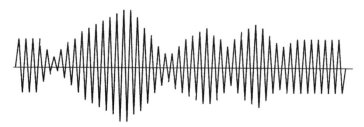

An *Amplitude Modulated* (AM) radio wave

amps　*see* A

AMVER　the *Atlantic Merchant Vessel Emergency Reporting System* was first established in 1958 as an Atlantic Ocean rescue program sponsored by the U.S. Coast Guard. It is a unique, computer-based, voluntary, global ship reporting system that provides the location of ships near a vessel in trouble and arranges for assistance by diverting the best-suited ship or ships to respond. In 1971 the service took on global proportions and its name was changed to the *Automated Mutual Assistance Vessel Rescue System*, while still retaining the same abbreviation, AMVER.

anch   a hydrographic abbreviation (not italicized) that is used in NOAA charts to indicate an *anchorage*.

ANT   an acronym for the U.S. Coast Guard's *Aids to Navigation Team*, which often uses *Trailerable Aids to Navigation Boats* (TANBs) to check on the correct location and operation of aids to navigation. *See also* TANB

AP   in navigation the *assumed position* is the hypothesized location of the observer, usually derived by *dead reckoning*. *See* DR

APBA   the abbreviation for the *American Powerboat Association* which, among other duties, manages many offshore powerboat races. In January 2005 they combined their resources with *Superboat International Productions* (SBIP) to promote the sport of offshore powerboat racing. The new organization, *World Powerboat Racing, Inc.* (WPR) has a ten year licensing agreement with the *American Powerboat Racing Association*. *See also* SBIP; WPR

AR   an abbreviation for *aspect ratio*, which relates the vertical line (height) to the horizontal. For sailboats, the *aspect ratio* can be either a hull's below-water shape or the shape of the sails. In both cases, everything else being equal, the higher the *aspect ratio*, the better windward performance.

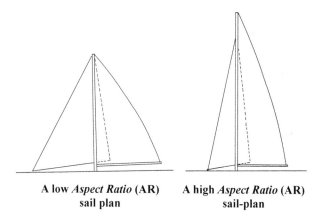

A low *Aspect Ratio* (AR) sail plan   **A high *Aspect Ratio* (AR) sail-plan**

ARPA *Automatic Radar Plotting Aids* give marine radars the ability to follow the targets of other vessels, calculate their course, speed, *closest point of approach* (CPA), and the *time of closest point of approach* (TCPA). The development of ARPA began in the 1960s after the ANDREA DORIA disaster. Some companies call this radar feature *ATA*, for *Automatic Tracking Aid*. *See also* CPA; TCPA

ARPA *Advanced Research Projects Agency Network*, (ARPANET) which specifies interface standards for computers.

art an abbreviation used in NOAA charts to indicate an *articulating light*.

ASA the *American Sailing Association* has been an educator in U.S. sailing for two decades. It has more than

200 accredited sailing schools throughout the U.S., and more than 200,000 students have graduated from these training programs. The ASA has formed a partnership with the *U.S. Coast Guard*, the *State Boating Law Administrators' Education Committee*, the *Department of Transportation*, and the *National Park Service* in helping to make the sailing lifestyle safer and more enjoyable.

ASA   the *American Sportfishing Association* is the leading recreational fishing trade organization whose mission is to safeguard and promote the values of sportfishing.

ASMA   the *American Society of Marine Artists* was founded in 1978 as a non-profit, tax-exempt organization to promote marine art and encourage those in the marine art field.

ASMFC   the *Atlantic States Marine Fisheries Commission* was formed by the 15 Atlantic coastal states in 1942 to coordinate the conservation and management of the states' shared near-shore fishery resources for sustainable use.

ASTA   the *American Sail Training Association*, founded in 1973, is one of many national sail training organizations that coordinates and conducts sail training activities, primarily that of sailing and racing tall ships on the *International Sail Training Association* model.

ASTM   the *American Society for Testing and Materials* is over a hundred years old and is now known as *ASTM International*. It is one of the largest voluntary standards organizations. It develops standards for many products and industries worldwide. (For example, many boat engine manufacturers' warrantees specify that the fuel and oil used in their engines must meet ASTM standards).

ATA see ARPA

ATON the U.S. Coast Guard's abbreviation for *Aids to Navigation*.

AUTH an abbreviation used in NOAA charts to indicate *authorized*.

AW see AWA

AWA the *apparent wind angle* is the wind angle that is perceived on board. It is the resultant vector of a parallelogram whose sides are the *true wind* angle and speed, and the *wind of motion* angle and speed, created by the boat's movement through the air. *See also* TWS

az *Azimuth* is the great circle direction of any place or object from a given point and is chiefly used to designate the direction of a heavenly body in celestial navigation. *See also* Zn

B

b an abbreviation often used for *bearing*. Bearing is essentially the same as *azimuth* (Az), but is more commonly used in radar, radio direction-finding, or in visual sights. *Bearings* may be *true, magnetic, compass,* or *relative,* according to the reference point. *See also* Az

BA the *British Admiralty* is the agency which, among other things, is responsible for charting the waters of the United Kingdom.

bat a common abbreviation for *battery*. On an alternator the BAT terminal is the alternator's output charging current that is connected to the battery's positive terminal.

BC the common abbreviation for *Boat Club*.

BFO a *beat frequency oscillator* makes the presence of an unmodulated radio signal audible by beating together (heterodyning) two slightly different frequencies.

bk or ***brk*** an italicized qualifying term used as a hydrographic abbreviation on NOAA charts meaning *broken*.

bkw an abbreviation used in NOAA charts to indicate *breakwater*.

bl an italicized hydrographic abbreviation used in NOAA charts to indicate *black*.

BLDC (motors) *brushless DC* motors are high-efficiency DC motors that operate without a commutator, and generally use permanent magnets in place of the conventional field winding. They are the usual type of motor used in electrically-driven boats. See also DC

blds an italicized hydrographic abbreviation used in NOAA charts to indicate that the seabed at that point has *boulders*.

bn   an abbreviation used in NOAA charts to indicate a *beacon*. It may also be used with a qualifying term (i.e. Bn Tr, for *beacon tower*).

BNC   a radio frequency (r.f.) and video coaxial cable connector, named for its "bayonet" locking mechanism and its two inventors, Neill and Concelman. It is commonly used on electronic equipment and is an alternative to the RCA connector.

BoatU.S.   the *Boat Owners Association of the United States* offers savings and service to millions of U.S. boat owners, and is the nation's most powerful advocate for advancing the interests of boaters. BoatU.S. offers extensive and comprehensive information on their website and in the monthly BoatU.S. Magazine, retail sales discounts from either their on-line store or through West Marine stores, boat and towing insurance, governmental lobbying programs, safety and awareness programs and alerts, and a host of other services for the recreational boater.

BOC Challenge   a 27,000 mile, solo, around the world yacht race that takes place every four years. It was originally sponsored by the *British Oxygen Corporation*. The route leaves all the Capes to port, with four mandatory stopovers along the way. In 1990 the race was named the *Around Alone*. In 2006, it has been renamed the *VELUX 5 Oceans Race*.

BPO   *benzoyle-peroxide* is a catalyst used to initiate the cure of certain polyester and vinylester-styrene resins that are used for fillers, patching, or putties.

br an abbreviation used in NOAA charts to indicate *breakers*.

brk see bk

BSB the standard Windows-based format for downloading charts into a navigational software program that runs on a personal computer. This standard was co-developed by NOAA and Maptech.

bu an italicized hydrographic abbreviation used in NOAA charts to indicate *blue*.

BUI an abbreviation for *boating under the influence*. See also BWI

BWHB an abbreviation used in NOAA charts to indicate *black and white horizontal bands*.

BWI an abbreviation for *Boating Writers International*, whose active members are writers, photographers, and broadcasters, and whose associate and supporting members are public relations or communications firms, as well as manufacturers and publishers in the boating field.

BWI an abbreviation for *boating while intoxicated*. See also BUI

BWVS an abbreviation used in NOAA charts to indicate *black and white vertical stripes*.

C

C is used to indicate *celsius (centigrade)*; *chronometer time*; *compass direction*; *correction*; or a vessel's *course*.

c an abbreviation (not italicized) that is used in NOAA charts to indicate a *cove*.

c an italicized qualifying term used as a hydrographic abbreviation on NOAA charts meaning *coarse*, and can be used in conjunction with the hydrographic abbreviation *S*, for *sand*, to indicate the size of the sand particles. (i.e. *cS*).

ca an italicized qualifying term used on NOAA charts, meaning *calcareous*, and used in conjunction with another hydrographic abbreviation that indicates bottom composition.

CAN or **CANbus** or **CAN bus** a network implemented in the hardware of many types of marine electronics, and consisting of multiple microcontrollers that need to communicate with each other.

CASP the *Computer Assisted Search Planning System* has been designed and developed to help Search and Rescue controllers manage information, plan searches, and obtain results easily and quickly.

CB or **C_B** the *center of buoyancy* of a boat is the center of gravity of the water displaced by the hull. With a boat floating level, this C_B is on the centerline, below the *center of gravity* (C_G), but when the boat heels, the C_B

moves to one side, while the center of gravity remains the same. The horizontal distance between the two is the *righting arm* (GZ). See Cg; GZ

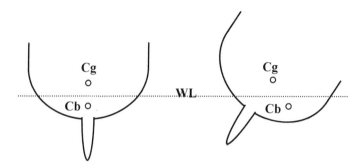

The relationship between *Center of Gravity* (Cg) and *Center of Buoyancy* (Cb)

CB   an abbreviation for *centerboard*.

CB   an abbreviation for the *Citizen's Band radio service*, which is a public, two-way personal radio service with 40 channels which requires no FCC license and operates in a band near 27 MHz.

cb   an italicized hydrographic abbreviation used in NOAA charts to indicate that the seabed at that point is composed of *cobbles*.

CBTF   the *canting ballast twin foil* is the cutting edge of racing sailboat technology. It consists of a canting strut with a bulb of ballast at its tip, and fore and aft controllable foils, or rudders, to affect changes in side force and for maneuvering.

CBTF   the abbreviation for the *Chesapeake Bay Triton Fleet*.

CCA the *Cruising Club of America* was launched in the winter of 1921-22 and designed to promote improved seamanship, the design of safe yachts and safe yachting practices, and environmental awareness.

CCA an abbreviation for the *cold cranking amps* of a battery. It is the number of amps a 12-volt battery can deliver for 30 seconds at 0° F. while maintaining its voltage above 7.2 volts. *See also* MCA

CCTV on board recreational vessels, *closed circuit TV* cameras are often used under-water, as well as in other key locations, and are usually viewed on a *multi-function display* (MFD).

CD the *Chart Datum* or *Chart Sounding Datum*. It determines the position of the latitude and longitude overlays on a chart. On current U.S. charts the horizontal reference *datum* is the *North American Datum of 1983* (NAD 83) which is considered to be the equivalent of the *World Geodetic System* 1984 (WGS 84). This is the default *datum* setting for most GPS receivers sold in the U.S. When a GPS receiver is used with charts of a different *datum* (such as older US charts or charts outside the U.S.) the GPS receiver's *datum* must be reset accordingly. Failure to reset the GPS *datum* in these cases can result in a position fix that is incorrect.

CD *Chart Datum* is the reference water level to which tide heights are measured.

C&D an abbreviation for the *Chesapeake and Delaware Canal*, a 12-mile-long man-made canal with no locks and no tolls that connects the Delaware River with the north end of Chesapeake Bay.

CDI on electronic navigation displays CDI is an abbreviation for *course deviation indicator*, or the amount of divergence from the intended course.

CDMA an abbreviation for *code-division multiple access*, a digital cellular phone technology that uses "spread-spectrum" techniques, unlike competing systems, such as GSM. *See also* GSM; TDMA

CE or **C$_E$** in naval architecture, the *center of effort* on a sail, or a combination of sails, is calculated by the geometric center of the individual or aggregate sail-shapes. In reality, the true *center of effort* on a sail or sails is displaced somewhat from the geometric center and also changes position with every change in sail trim.

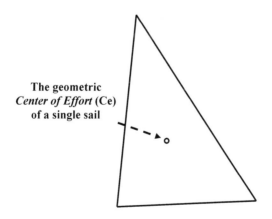

The geometric *Center of Effort* (Ce) of a single sail

CE *chronometer error* in celestial navigation.

CE   an abbreviation for *compass error*, which is the algebraic sum of *variation* and *deviation*. *See also* Dev; Var

CE   a marking that is a declaration by the manufacturer that the product meets all the appropriate provisions of the relevant legislation implementing certain European Directives. The CE marking gives boat and boat-equipment manufacturers easier access into the European market to sell their products without adaptation or rechecking.

CEDRA   an acronym for the *Center for Documentation, Research, and Experimentation into Accidental Pollution of the Water*.

CF   the *center of flotation* of a hull is the geometric center of the area of the hull at the waterline. It is the point about which the vessel pivots.

CG or **C_G**   the *center of gravity* is an important element in yacht design. It is the point from which a mass can be suspended in equilibrium in any position. *See also* Cb

CG   is sometimes used as an abbreviation for *Coast Guard*, however USCG is more common.

CGC   the Coast Guard's abbreviation for *Coast Guard Cutter*.

CGDONE   the Coast Guard's abbreviation for *Coast Guard District One*. Other Coast Guard Districts follow a similar abbreviation pattern.

CHY or **chy**   an abbreviation used in NOAA charts to indicate a *chimney*.

CIO   the *Central Imaging Office*. See NGA

CI   see Cy

CI   a non-italicized abbreviation used in NOAA charts to indicate *clearance*.

CLP   the *center of lateral plane* is similar to the *center of lateral resistance (CLR)*. See CLR

CLR or **C$_L$**   the *center of lateral resistance* or the *center of lateral plane* is a naval architectural term. It is assumed to be the geometric center of a boat's underwater profile with the boat floating upright and on its lines. Sometimes, the rudder area is omitted from this area. In practice, a boat that is heeling or one that is rolling and/or pitching has a *center of lateral resistance* that is constantly changing.

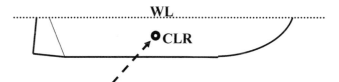

The *Center of Lateral Resistance* **(CLR)**
is the **geometric center of the underwater profile of a hull**

CMC   the *Center for Marine Conservation* is a non-profit advocacy group committed to protecting the ocean environment and marine life through citizen participation.

CMG the *course made good* is the net resultant direction of movement from one point to another, disregarding the inaccuracies of steering and the effect of wind and currents. *See also* COG

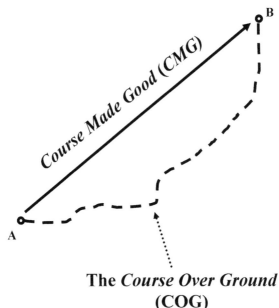

The *Course Over Ground* (COG)

CNC a *computer numerical control* machine is a manufacturing tool that can be programmed to create products that are identical and is often used in boat construction.

CNG *compressed natural gas* is stored in tanks under high pressure in its gaseous state. It is one of the safest galley-stove fuels, since it is lighter than air and will not accumulate in the bilge. Unfortunately, it is not readily available, especially outside of the U.S.

CO the chemical formula for *carbon monoxide*, which is a gas of one carbon atom and one oxygen atom. It is a gas

COLREGS

you can't smell, see, or taste, and is an extremely toxic substance that is potentially lethal. A *carbon monoxide* alarm should be part of the standard equipment on board.

CO_2 the chemical formula for *carbon dioxide*, which is an atmospheric gas composed of one carbon atom and two oxygen atoms. It is present in the earth's atmosphere in low concentrations and acts as a greenhouse gas. It is a major component of the carbon cycle.

co an italicized hydrographic abbreviation used in NOAA charts to indicate that the seabed at that point is *coral* or *coralline algae*.

COB an abbreviation for *crew overboard*. It is more politically correct than MOB (*man overboard*).

COE among their other duties, the U.S. Army *Corps of Engineers* manages hydropower facilities, coordinates dredging operations, and builds breakwaters and jetties.

COG *course over ground* is used in navigation to describe the actual path of the vessel across the surface of the earth. *See also* CMG

Co Hd an italicized hydrographic abbreviation used in NOAA charts to indicate that the seabed at that point has *coral head*(s).

COLREGS the *International Regulations for Preventing Collisions at Sea* is an agreement among maritime nations for the operation of vessels in international waters. In the US, these *International Rules of the Road* are published by the United States Coast Guard and distributed by the U.S.

Government Printing Office. These rules also delineate those waters upon which mariners shall comply with either the Inland or International Rules. In the U.K. these international rules are abbreviated as *IRPCS*.

COSPAS-SARSAT a satellite system designed to provide distress alert and location data to assist Search and Rescue (SAR) operations. Distress signals from an EPIRB are received by the COSPAS-SARSAT satellites and are relayed to a satellite ground station, or *local user terminal* (LUT). The information is then sent to a *mission control center* (MCC) which alerts the appropriate response team at a *rescue coordination center* (RCC). *See* EPIRB; LUT; MCC; RCC

COTP the Coast Guard's abbreviation for *Captain of the Port*.

CP or **Cp** or **PC** the *prismatic coefficient* is the naval architect's term for how fine or how full is the shape of a hull. More precisely, it is the ratio between the volume of displacement of a hull and another solid with the same waterline length but having a constant section the shape of the hull's largest section.

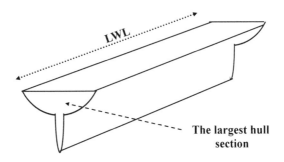

One of the measurements used to determine the *Prismatic Coefficient* (Cp or PC) of a hull

CQR

CPA when plotting courses, CPA is the predicted *closest point of approach* to another boat, or obstacle. *See also* ARPA; TCPA

CPFV a *commercial passenger fishing vessel*, such as a charter boat.

cps *cycles per second* is a term in electronics that has largely been replaced with the single word *Hertz* (Hz). *See* Hz

CQD this was the first international distress call established in 1904. CQ was the call for all stations, and *D* was for distress. It was replaced in 1908 when *SOS* became the internationally-recognized distress call. When the *Titanic* sank in 1912, it sent out both *CQD* and *SOS* distress signals. *See also* SOS

CQR the name for a patented type of galvanized, drop-forged, high-tensile steel, plow anchor, which includes a trip-line eye. A genuine CQR is often the choice of blue water cruisers due to its good holding power in a variety of bottoms. The letters, CQR, are phonetic for *secure*.

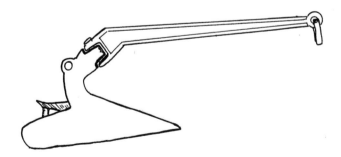

The CQG anchor

cr a hydrographic abbreviation (not italicized) that is used in NOAA charts to indicate a *creek*.

CROPBRA an abbreviation for the *Conch Republic Offshore Powerboat Racing Association*, which is the organizer of offshore powerboat races in Key West.

CR the *common rail* is a diesel injection system that uses very high pressure with electronically-controlled piezoelectric injectors. Whereas, in a normal diesel, the fuel-injection pump, driven by the camshaft, delivers pulses of fuel to each injector in turn, a *common rail* diesel maintains high fuel pressure to all the injectors, which are turned on and off electronically. The result is increased power with fewer unwanted exhaust emissions.

CRT the *cathode ray tube* was originally used to display images for Loran, radar, television, and computer monitors. Due to the CRT's high power requirements, high operating voltage, size, and fragility, the CRT has largely been replaced on recreational boats by the *liquid crystal display* (LCD) or the *thin film display* (TFD). *See also* LCD; TFD

CSA the *Canadian Standards Association* is a not-for-profit, membership-based association that develops standards, such as those for enhancing public safety and health, helping to preserve the environment, and facilitate trade.

CUP or **Cup** an abbreviation used in NOAA charts to indicate a *cupola*.

CUT *Coordinated Universal Time. See* UTC

CVA in 1962 the *Clean Vessel Act* was passed by Congress to help reduce pollution from vessel sewage discharges. The program funds 100% of the cost of installing a pump-out station at marinas and public facilities. Pump-outs installed with funding from CVA must be open to the public, cost no more than $5 to use, and be accessible to all boaters.

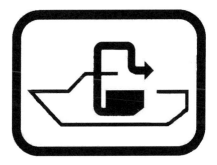

The standardized logo above identifies a Pump-Out Station

C_W in naval architecture the *waterplane coefficient*, or *fineness coefficient* is a coefficient of comparison between the horizontal area occupied by the hull at the waterline to the area of a rectangle with the same length and width as the hull.

CW *continuous wave* is a term used when *Morse code* is transmitted by radio. The transmitter's unmodulated *continuous wave* is turned on and off with the operator's telegraph key. *CW Morse code* is no longer used by the U.S. Coast Guard or ships at sea. *See also* BFO

The CW radio wave of Morse Code letter "A" (dot-dash)

CWA the *Federal Water Pollution Control Act* is commonly known as the *Clean Water Act*. It establishes the basic structure for regulating discharges of pollutants into U.S. waters.

cy an italicized hydrographic abbreviation used in NOAA charts to indicate that the seabed at that point is *clay*.

CYA the *Canadian Yachting Association*, formed in 1931, was originally part of the *North American Yacht Racing Union* (NAYRU). In 1975 the NAYRU changed its name to the USYRU, the *United States Yacht Racing Union*, and its Canadian counterpart became the *Canadian Yachting Association* (CYA). See USYRU

D

D an abbreviation sometimes used for *deviation*, although *Dev* is more common. See Dev

dB *decibels* is a unit for measuring the logarithmic intensity of electrical, electromagnetic, or sound energy.

dBZ a term used in weather radar, which is the measure of the radar reflection, with dB(decibels) indicating intensity and Z denoting reflectivity. In general, the higher the dBZ (or the intensity of the reflected radar beam) the greater the indicated precipitation. Measurable precipitation normally begins at about 15 dBZ, while values of about 40 dBZ indicate heavy thunderstorms. See also dB

DCI see DCS

DCS *decompression sickness* happens when inert gases (mainly nitrogen) that are normally dissolved in body fluids and tissues form gaseous bubbles. This happens when the body is exposed to decreased pressures. It is analogous to the bubbles formed when the top of a soda bottle is removed. If this decreased pressure happens too suddenly, in the case of a SCUBA diver ascending too fast from a dive, the bubbles formed can cause rashes, joint pain (the "bends"), sensory failure, paralysis, and death. Air embolism, caused by another process, can have the same symptoms, and the two conditions are grouped together under the name *decompression illness* (DCI). *See also* SCUBA

DCT with *depth contour tracking*, an autopilot interfaced to a compatible depthsounder can be programmed to steer the vessel along a specific depth contour.

DDPO the *Defense Dissemination Program Office*. *See* NGA

Dec an abbreviation for *declination*. The *declination* of a celestial body is the latitude of the point on the earth where that body is directly overhead, or the point where a line between that body and the center of the Earth, enters the Earth's surface. *See also* GP

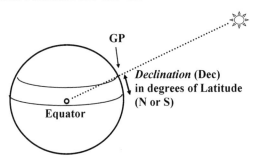

Dev the abbreviation for *deviation*, which is sometimes also abbreviated with *D*. Every boat has its particular influences on the vessel's compass. These influences are caused by ferrous metals, magnets, electric currents, and electronic equipment on board. These cause a difference between the compass bearing and the true magnetic bearing. It is different for every boat and changes with the boat's heading and angle of heel. This difference is called *Deviation (Dev)*. The algebraic sum of *Deviation* and *Variation* is *Compass Error*. See also Var

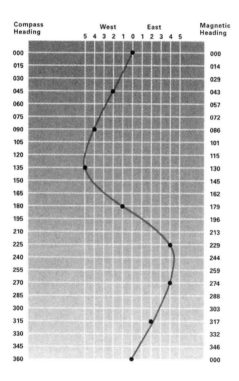

Every boat should have a *Deviation* chart. This is a typical *one*.

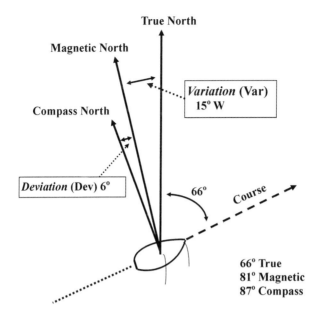

Showing the relationship of
Deviation (Dev) and *Variation* (Var)

DF a radio *direction finder. See* RDF

DF for an alternator. *See* FLD

DGPS the *Differential Global Positioning System*. When initially put into service, the GPS system was so accurate that the Department of Defense deliberately introduced an error into the civilian GPS system to prevent its use by terrorists. However this error, *Selective Availability* (SA), caused a potential hazard to users. If a boat were coming through a narrow inlet in a fog, the error that was introduced by *Selective Availability* could put it on the rocks. So the Coast Guard established low-frequency AM ground stations along the coast, and accessing the data from one of these stations would take out the error introduced by the Department of Defense. This DGPS system requires a separate antenna system and receiver, as well as a GPS receiver that is equipped and programmed for a DGPS input. In May 2000, the *Selective Availability* error was discontinued, and overnight GPS users worldwide had a dramatically more accurate system.

But there were still potential errors in the system—such as clock errors; ionospheric and tropospheric delays as the signal travels from the satellites to earth; earth reflections; satellite orbital drifts; and control errors. The DGPS ground stations' corrections could reduce most of these errors. But the DGPS ground stations had limited range, and were subject to noise and fading, so geostationary satellites, operating in the same frequency band as the GPS satellites, were put in orbit, and these "stationary" satellites provide corrections that can be received directly on a GPS antenna. This improved correction system is known as the *Wide Area Augmentation System* (WAAS). *See also* GPS; WAAS.

dk an italicized abbreviation used in NOAA charts to indicate *dark*.

Dk a non-italicized abbreviation used in NOAA charts to indicate *dock*.

DLWL the *designed length of the waterline* of a boat is the waterline as shown on the designer's drawing board. It may be the same as the actual *length of the waterline* (LWL) when the boat is in the water, but usually it is not, since added equipment, and soaking of the wood in a wooden boat, settles the hull lower in the water, changing her waterline length. *See* LWL.

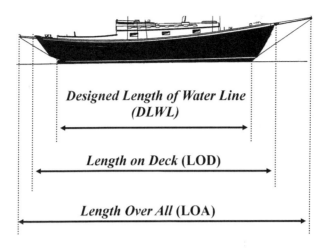

DMA see DMAHC; NGA

DMAHC the *Defense Mapping Agency Hydrographic Center* is charged with the production of charts for the waters of the world, except for the United States, either from its own field work or from the charts of other nations. Charts for U.S. waters are prepared by the *National Ocean Survey*. The *Defense Mapping Agency* (DMA) is part of the *Defense Department's National Geospatial-Intelligence Agency*. See also NOS

DN (Iceboat) the *DN* is the largest iceboat class in the world. It was so named because it was the winner of an iceboat design contest sponsored by the *Detroit News (DN)* in 1937.

Dn or **Dns** or **Dol** an abbreviation used in NOAA charts to indicate *dolphin(s)*. A *dolphin* is a bundle of pilings tied together to form either the base for a navigational aid or a bumper for pier or slip protection.

DNR individual state governments have a *Department of Natural Resources*, which monitors and regulates that state's natural resources on both land and water.

DO *dissolved oxygen* in the water is necessary for the survival of fish as well as all other aerobic, aquatic animals and plants. In water quality tests *DO* is measured in parts-per-million (ppm). Arthropods and fish have well developed gills that are able to extract this tiny percentage of dissolved oxygen from the water.

DoD or **DOD** the U.S. Government's *Department of Defense*.

DOI the U.S. *Department of the Interior*.

DOT the U.S. *Department of Transportation* is involved in establishing standards for land and sea, including marine and recreational boating.

DP *see* DPS

DPDT a *double pole double throw* electrical switch is a switch where two separate circuits can each access two other circuits simultaneously. *See also* SPST; SPDT; SPDTCO; DPST

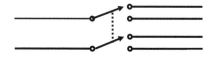

**Schematic Diagram for a
Double Pole Double Throw (DPDT) switch**

DPDTCO a *double pole double throw center off* electrical switch is a DPDT switch with a "center-off" position. *See* DPDT

DPS the *dynamic positioning system* is a specialized positioning system that is primarily used on very large or special-purpose boats. Its basic function is to make a vessel hold its position using propulsion and thrusters.

DPST a *double pole single throw* electrical switch is a switch where two separate circuits can be turned on or off simultaneously. *See also* SPST; SPDT; SPDTCO; DPDT; DPDTCO

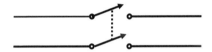

Schematic diagram for a
***Double Pole Single Throw* (DPST) switch**

DR *dead reckoning* is thought to have originally been an abbreviation for *deduced reckoning,* or *ded. reckoning.* It is the probable, or approximate, position of the vessel as determined by plotting the course steered, the boat's speed, the elapsed time, and the effects of wind and currents.

DSC when using VHF-FM, *digital selective calling* allows the operator, at the touch of a single button, to transmit an automatic MAYDAY call, which includes the *maritime mobile service identification number* (MMSI) describing the vessel in distress. Also, through an interface with an external or internal GPS, the latitude and longitude can also be automatically transmitted. In addition, DSC can be used for making direct phone calls without going through the marine operator, or ship-to-ship calls to other DSC-equipped vessels. A DSC-equipped radio must be registered with the FCC, which can be done easily through *BoatU.S.* The MMSI number for each of these radios is similar to a telephone number, so when making a DSC ship-to-ship call, you must know the MMSI number of the other party. *See* BoatU.S.; MMSI; VHF-FM

DSL   a *digital subscriber line* is a very high speed connection that uses the same wires as a regular telephone line to connect to the Internet.

DSS   a *digital satellite system* is a small-dish satellite receiver used for receiving television programs.

DTS   an abbreviation for *digital throttle and shift* system. It replaces the mechanical cables with an electrical harness through which digital signals are sent electronically from the helm to control the engine.

DVB   the *Digital Video Broadcasting* Project (DVB) is an industry-led consortium of over 270 broadcasters, manufacturers, network operators, software developers, regulatory bodies and others in over 35 countries committed to designing global standards for the global delivery of digital television and data services.

DWL   *see* DLWL

DZ an abbreviation used in NOAA charts to indicate *danger zone*.

E

E *East* is one of the cardinal directional points. It is represented as 90 degrees, and may be either referenced to Compass, Magnetic, or True *North*. *See also* Var

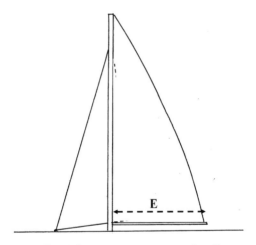

The "E" measurement on a mainsail

E in sail measurement, "E" is the length of the foot of the mainsail, along the boom, from the tack to the clew of the sail. For the mizzen sail of a ketch or yawl this measurement is defined as *Ey*.

EBL on a radar display, the *electronic bearing line* is the relative bearing to a target, measured in degrees.

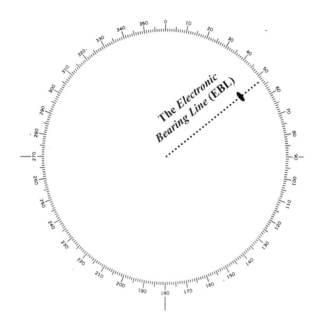

E by N *East by North* is a compass direction. Today, directions are measured on a 360-degree scale with North as the reference, however in older times this 360 degrees was subdivided into 32 *points*, with one *point* equaling 11.25 degrees. These points were named, not numbered. The *point* system is now nearly obsolete, except when occasionally used to describe wind directions. E by N equals 78.75 degrees or 78 degrees 45 minutes. It may be referenced either to Compass, Magnetic, or True North. *See also* Var

E by S *East by South* is a compass direction. E by S equals 101.25 degrees or 101 degrees 15 minutes. *See E by N*

ECB an *electronic circuit breaker* offers many advantages over magnetic or thermal circuit breakers. Its internal

EGNOS 37

microprocessor is programmable, allowing changes in parameters, including over-current trip amperage.

ECDIS the *electronic chart display and information system* is a navigational tool that displays electronic charts on a screen, usually using a Liquid Crystal Display (LCD) or a *thin film transistor* (TFT) display in a manner that complies with accepted standards. *See also* ECS; ENC; RCDS

ECS a general term for an *electronic chart system*, which usually denotes a system that does not necessarily conform to ECDIS and RCDS standards. *See also* ECDIS; ENC; RCDS

ECU the *electronic control unit* is a microprocessor that receives information about the engine's operation (fuel injection, ignition timing, idling speed, air flow, coolant temperature, etc.) and determines the optimum settings that control these functions. Although once only found on very large engines, smaller engines are now beginning to use this technology.

EEZ the *exclusive economic zone* extends typically to 200 miles off the coast of a nation or half way between two nations whose coast lines are close together. It is in this area that a nation claims economic control for such activities as seafood harvesting.

EFI *electronic fuel injection* is superior to carburetors as a fuel supply system.

EGNOS the *European Geostationary Navigation Overlay Service* uses three geostationary satellites to augment the two satellite navigational systems now operating, the *U.S. GPS* and the Russian *Glonass* systems. It provides correctional information for Europe, similar to the U.S. *WAAS* geostationary satellite system. *See* GLONASS; GPS; WAAS

ELC *extended life coolant* is an anti-freeze that uses *carboxylates* to slow the coolant's transition into acid. In diluting ELC, distilled water should be used, since the minerals in tap water can build up scale in the heat-exchanger of an engine using *ELC*.

eLED the *edge-emitting LED* is a light-emitting diode with an output that emanates from between the heterogeneous layers. It provides longer bulb life, greater radiance, and is much more durable and impact-resistant than a conventional LED. *See also* LED; TFT

EMI or **EMI/RFI** EMI is an abbreviation for *electromagnetic interference* and RFI is an abbreviation for *radio frequency interference*. EMI and RFI are interferences emitted by electrical devices that cause other electronic devices to malfunction. Many countries have legislation and standards to govern and minimize these unwanted and interfering emissions.

EMT the Coast Guard's abbreviation for *emergency medical technician*.

ENC a government-authorized data-base with a standardized format for *electronic navigational charts*.

EPIRB 39

ENE *East North East* is a compass direction. *ENE* equals 67.50 degrees or 67 degrees 30 minutes. *See E by N*

EPA the *Environmental Protection Agency* has, since 1970, been charged with protecting the environment and human health.

EPIRB an acronym for *Emergency Position Indicating Radio Beacon*. Early EPIRBs operated on 121.5 MHz, a frequency designed for detection by aircraft before satellite availability. This frequency was not ideal for a satellite system, and a newer EPIRB system, operating on 406.025 MHz, provides global coverage, is more reliable, and includes better vessel data. The EPIRB's automatic, emergency transmitter sends a *unique identification number* (UIN) to the COSPAS-SARSAT satellite *search and rescue* (SAR) system. The UIN, which has previously been registered with the Coast Guard, identifies the vessel in trouble. This information, along with the vessel's location, is then received at a local user terminal (LUT) which is a satellite ground station. The information goes to a mission control center (MCC), and then to a rescue coordination center (RCC), from which the physical rescue operations is deployed. The position of a 406 MHz EPIRB is determined by using doppler shift, which takes time for an accurate fix to be acquired. GPIRB is an EPIRB with an internal GPS which transmits an accurate fix almost instantly without the inherent delay of the doppler-shift location process. On February 1, 2009 the search and rescue COSPAS-SARSAT satellite program will terminate its processing of distress signals on 121.5 MHz. *See also* COSPAS-SARSAT; GEOSAR; GPS; LUT; MCC; RCC; UIN

ER an abbreviation for the *engine room*.

ESA the *Endangered Species Act* is administered by the *Fish and Wildlife Service*, in the *Department of the Interior*, and the *National Oceanic and Atmospheric Administration (NOAA) Fisheries*.

ESE *East South East* is a compass direction. *ESE* equals 112.5 degrees or 112 degrees 30 minutes. *See E by N*

ETA the *estimated time of arrival*.

EVRM *see* VRM

Ey *see* E

F

F a non-italicized abbreviation used in NOAA charts to indicate *fixed*. *See also* FLD

F for an alternator. *See* FLD.

f an italicized qualifying term meaning *fine*, which is used with another hydrographic abbreviation on NOAA charts to provide additional information about the seabed at that point. (i.e. *fS* would indicate *fine sand*).

Facty an abbreviation used in NOAA charts to indicate *factory*.

FM

FCC the *Federal Communications Commission* is the government agency which, among other duties, regulates all radio transmissions in the United States.

FF when describing electronic equipment onboard, this term indicates that the boat is equipped with a *fish finder*.

FG *fiberglass* construction uses a relatively low strength resin, reinforced and made stronger with internal fibers of various types. The most common of these fibers is glass, although Kevlar and graphite fibers are also sometimes used. The plastics, mainly polymers, but sometimes epoxy or vinylesters, are usually of a thermosetting type. *See* FRP; GRP

Fl an abbreviation used in NOAA charts to indicate a *flashing light*.

FLD or **DF** or **F** the designation on an alternator for *field*. It is the input from the voltage regulator which controls alternator output current.

Fm or **fm** or **fms** on old sailing ships the *fathom* was a convenient measurement— it represented the length between outstretched arms. It was eventually established at 6 feet or 1.83 meters, or approximately one-thousandth of a nautical mile. It is generally used for depth soundings on offshore charts, but in many countries is being replaced by metric measurements.

FM *frequency modulation* is the modulation, or change, in the frequency of a radio wave in accordance with the strength of an audio or other signal that conveys information.

A *Frequency Modulation* (FM) radio wave

fne see f

FRP *fiberglass reinforced plastic.* See FG; GRP.

FRS the *family radio service* is a relatively new class of two-way radios intended for personal, non-commercial, limited range use. FRS radios do not require a FCC license and are a handy item for the boater when the use of a hand-held VHF marine radio is illegal, such as when onshore and communicating back to your boat.

Fsh Stks an abbreviation used in NOAA charts to indicate *fishing stakes*.

FTC on a radar display, the *fast time constant* is synonymous with "rain and snow clutter suppression."

FTP *file transfer protocol* is used to send files from local computers to distant computers and vice versa.

F/V the Coast Guard's abbreviation for *fishing vessel*.

FWC a term primarily used in boat advertisements to indicate that the boat's inboard engine is *fresh water cooled*. Fresh water cooling is an advantage in a salt water environment, since it extends the engine's life, and reduces corrosion of its internal passages.

G

G an abbreviation (not italicized) that is used in NOAA charts to indicate a *gulf*.

G in sail measurements, "G" is the *girth* of a spinnaker, measured from luff to luff, parallel to the foot, with the spinnaker spread flat.

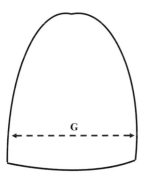

G an italicized hydrographic abbreviation used in NOAA charts to indicate that the seabed at that point is *gravel*.

GEO   *see* GEOSS

GEOLUT   *see* LUT

GEOSAR   the *Geostationary Search and Rescue* satellite constellation is part of the COMPAS-SARSAT satellite system. The *Geosar* system consists of geostationary satellites that are 406 MHz EPIRB repeaters. The system is only used for identification purposes, and the position information of the activated EPIRB is derived from the LEOSAR satellite system. *See also* COMPAS-SARSAT; EPIRB; LEOSAR; LUT; MCC; RCC

GEOSS the *Global Earth Observation System of Systems*. In April 2004, U.S. Cabinet members met with ministers from over 50 nations to create the GEOSS, which was originally begun as an ad hoc group called GEO (*Group on Earth Observations*). GEOSS's goal is to collect and disseminate data, information, and models, using compatible hardware and software, of air, land, and sea environmental observations and their interactions, to concerned government agencies and individuals worldwide.

GFI *see* GFCI

GFCI a *ground fault circuit interrupter*. It is an inexpensive electrical device that could prevent the majority of electrocutions each year. It interrupts the electric circuit when your body becomes an unintentional path to ground. Its use is especially important on boats, where nearly every piece of metal presents a path to ground.

GHA in celestial navigation the *Greenwich Hour Angle* is the hour angle measured between the celestial meridian of Greenwich and another meridian that has been projected onto the surface of the celestial sphere.

GHz *see* Hz

GLFC the *Great Lakes Fishery Commission* was established is 1955 by the Canadian/U.S. Convention on Great Lakes Fisheries to coordinate research, control the lamprey eel, and facilitate fishery management among the various agencies.

GLONASS the *Global Navigation Satellite System* is the Russian satellite navigation system that was born during

GMT 45

the days of the Cold War, primarily for military purposes. It is designed to be similar to GPS, but due to many delays the full 24 satellite system is now not scheduled to be completed till 2010.

GMDSS the *Global Maritime Distress and Safety System* is responsible for safety standards that are agreed to internationally. The GMDSS is specifically designed to automate a ship's radio distress alerting function and, as a consequence, removes the requirement for manual (human) watch-keeping on distress channels.

GMFMC the *Gulf of Mexico Fishery Management Council* is one of eight regional fishery management councils which were established by the Fishery Conservation and Management Act in 1976 (now called the Magnuson-Stevens Fishery Conservation and Management Act). The Council prepares fishery plans which are designed to manage fishery resources from where state waters end out to the 200-mile limit in the Gulf of Mexico. These waters are also known as the *Exclusive Economic Zone* (EEZ).

GMRS the two-way *general mobile radio service* can be used for either personal or business purposes. It uses relatively high power and operates in the UHF band. A $70 fee for a five year FCC license is required for operation.

GMT *Greenwich Mean Time* is the *Universal Time* accepted through much of the world. It is the time at the zero-degree meridian that passes through Greenwich, England. *See also* UTC

GMT the abbreviation for *Goetz Marine Technology*, or *GMT Composites, Inc*. It was one of the first companies to make extensive use of unidirectional carbon fiber for constructing rudders, quadrants, and spars.

gn an italicized hydrographic abbreviation used in NOAA charts to indicate *green*.

Gp an abbreviation used in NOAA charts to indicate *group* (i.e. Gp Fl for *group flashing*; Gp Occ for *group occulting*).

GP in celestial navigation the *geographical position* of a celestial body is the point on the surface of the Earth where that body is directly overhead, or the point where a line between that body and the center of the Earth, enters the Earth's surface.

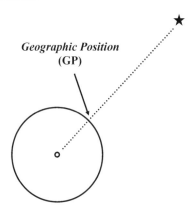

GPH an abbreviation for *gallons per hour*, usually used in describing fuel consumption.

GPIRB GPIRB is an EPIRB with an internal GPS which transmits an accurate fix almost instantly without the inherent delay of the doppler-shift location process. *See also* EPIRB; GPS

GPM an abbreviation for *gallons per minute*, usually used in describing a water-pump's capacity.

GPS the NAVSTAR *Global Positioning System* became fully operational in 1995. The *Global Positioning System* is a satellite navigation system that was designed for and is operated by the *Department of Defense* (*DoD*), but it is now used by millions of commercial organizations and civilians world-wide. The basic space segment of this system, known as the *GPS Operational Constellation*, consists of at least 24 operational satellites that orbit the earth twice a day. These satellites are in six separate orbits, with a minimum of four satellites traveling in each of the six orbital paths. These six orbits are spaced around the equator 60 degrees apart, and their orbital planes are canted about 55 degrees to the equatorial plane. Thus, this GPS constellation configuration provides the user at any point on earth with five or more visible satellites at any time. Each GPS satellite contains an atomic clock, and by measuring the time interval between the transmission and reception of a satellite signal, a spherical *line-of-position* (LOP) is created around each satellite. The intersection of these spherical lines-of-position determines location. Accuracy of the GPS system can be greatly improved with a receiver that can access the correctional data from the geostationary satellites of the *wide area augmentation system* (WAAS) or the *differential GPS* (DGPS) system. *See also* DGPS; LOP; WAAS

GPS Interface the ability of a GPS receiver to communicate its information to another piece of electronic navigational gear. *See also* NMEA

GRD a common abbreviation for an electrical *ground*.

GRP *glassfibre reinforced plastic* (U.K.). In the United States, FG, or FRP is used to describe this process. *See* FG

Grs an italicized hydrographic abbreviation used in NOAA charts to indicate that the seabed at that point has *grass*.

Gru the Coast Guard's abbreviation for *group*.

GSM a GSM phone is a type of mobile phone that uses the *Global System for Mobile Communications* to send and receive phone calls. GSM is a digital standard first offered in 1991 and is currently the most popular mobile phone technology in the world.

GZ in naval architecture GZ defines the mathematical *righting arm* which tries to push against the force that is making a boat heel. The greater this *righting arm*, the greater is the stability at a given angle of heel. *See also* Cb; Cg; WL

H

H on meteorological weather charts H indicates the center of a *high pressure system*. *See also* L

h an italicized qualifying hydrographic term used on NOAA charts, meaning *hard*. It is used in conjunction with another hydrographic abbreviation. (i.e *h*M, for *hard mud*).

h a non-italicized abbreviation used in NOAA charts to indicate *hour*.

HC *hydrocarbons* are an unwanted emission from internal combustion engines. Current regulations prescribe the maximum amount of these emissions (as of 2005) and it's probable that stricter regulations in the near future will require the use of catalytic converters in the exhaust systems to meet those new standards. The catalytic converter, a honeycomb of ceramic coated with platinum, rhodium, or palladium, burns the hydrocarbons (HC) and carbon monoxide (CO) to form water and oxygen. Engines so equipped will have to have sophisticated diagnostics, adding expense and complexity. In addition, the catalytic converter runs extremely hot, creating a safety issue in a confined engine compartment.

HD the abbreviation *HD* stands for *high definition*, when referring to display screen clarity.

Hdg the *heading* (*Hdg*) is the direction a vessel points or heads at any given instant, expressed in angular degrees. The *heading* is constantly changing due to steering errors and the effects of the sea. The *heading* is also sometimes abbreviated as *SH*, the *ship's heading*.

Helo the Coast Guard's abbreviation for *helicopter*.

HF in the electromagnetic spectrum *high frequency* specifies those frequencies between 3 and 30 megahertz (MHz). *See also* Hz

HIN the *hull identification number* is a set of twelve alpha-numeric characters imbedded in the upper, starboard side of the transom. The HIN is similar to the 17-character automobile's *vehicle identification number* (VIN). In the U.S., all boats that were either manufactured or imported after November 1, 1972, including home-built boats, are required by law to have a HIN. Since its inception there have been three different formats for the HIN: the 1972 "Straight Year" format; the 1972 "Model Year" format; and the 1984 "New Format."

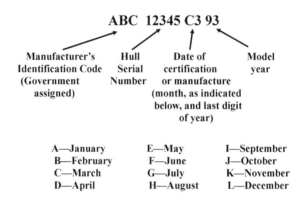

The most recent of the HIN formats, the "1984 New Format"

ABC 12345 C3 93

Manufacturer's Identification Code (Government assigned)

Hull Serial Number

Date of certification or manufacture (month, as indicated below, and last digit of year)

Model year

A—January   E—May   I—September
B—February   F—June   J—October
C—March   G—July   K—November
D—April   H—August   L—December

Note: Spaces shown in the example are only for explanation purposes. There are no spaces in the HIN.

HMPE   a *high modulus polyethylene* line is more commonly known by the trade names *Spectra* and *Dyneema*. This line is a high strength (high modulus), low stretch synthetic fiber that resists weathering and abrasion much better than *Polyester* (*Dacron*) line. This expensive line is used primarily for running rigging and is second only to *PBO* in strength. *See* PBO

HMS or **H.M.S.**   the prefix placed before the name of a warship of the British Navy. It came into use in the late 1700s and is an abbreviation for *Her Majesty's Ship* or *His Majesty's Ship*.

HMS   the abbreviation for the *highly migratory species* division of the *National Marine Fisheries Service* which manages Atlantic migratory fish, with international cooperation, consistent with other laws governing those migratory species.

Ho   in celestial navigation this is the *observed altitude* of a celestial body in degrees. Ho is the result of a sextant altitude observation (Hs) with all the necessary corrections applied. *See* Hs

HO   most countries around the world have their own *Hydrographic Offices*, and in the U.S. the *Office of Coastal Survey* (OCS), which is part of the *National Oceanic and Atmospheric Administration* (NOAA), is responsible for nautical chart data, collecting hydrographic data and information programs, as well as for producing nautical charts for U.S. waters, its possessions, and territories. *See also* NOAA; OCS.

HO-229   a six-volume series of *Sight Reduction Tables for Marine Navigators*, with each of the six volumes covering 15 degrees of latitude. It is a U.S. Government publication that allows solving celestial navigation's spherical triangles with simple arithmetic.

HP, H.P., or **hp**   *horsepower* is a unit of power. In the *foot-pound-second* (f.p.s.) system (used in the U.S.), one-hp raises 1 lb. 500 feet-per second. In the *metric* system one-hp raises 75 kg one meter per second. When describing boat engines, *indicated horsepower* is the power developed in the cylinders; *brake horsepower* is the power measured at the engine's output shaft—and is less than *indicated horsepower* due to mechanical losses in the engine; and *shaft horsepower* is the power delivered to the propeller shaft, and is lower than both *indicated horsepower* and *brake horsepower*.

hrd   see h

Hs   in celestial navigation Hs is the altitude of a body above the visible horizon as read from the sextant's scale before the necessary corrections are applied. *See also* Ho

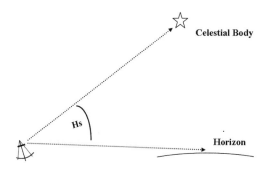

Hz   in designating frequencies in the electromagnetic spectrum, *Hertz* (Hz) means *cycle(s)-per-second*. kHz (kilo-Hertz) represents 1,000 cycles per second; MHz (mega-Hertz) represents a million cycles per second; and GHz (Giga-Hertz) represents a billion cycles per second. The word is in honor of Heinrich Hertz, a physicist who studied the properties of electric waves in the late 1800s.

I

I in sail measurement, "I" is the height of the foretriangle, where the jib or spinnaker is hoisted, measured along the foreside of the mast from the main deck to the top of the jib halyard or spinnaker halyard sheave.

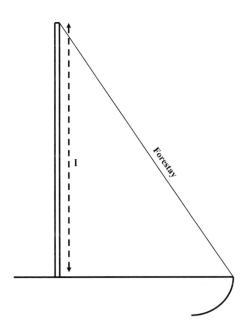

IALA the *International Association of Lighthouse Authorities* is an international, non-profit association, established in 1957 to encourage its members to work toward harmonizing aids to navigation worldwide, and for the development of common standards.

IB an abbreviation used mostly in advertising copy to indicate that a boat has an *inboard* engine.

IC in celestial navigation the *index correction* is the correction which must be applied to the altitude measured (Hs) using a sextant, due to that individual sextant's inherent mechanical errors. *See also* Ho; Hs

ICC the *International Coastal Cleanup* is an organization of 118 countries whose volunteers, since 1986, have removed over 78 million pounds of debris from over 114,000 miles of coastline.

ICCAT the *International Commission for the Conservation of Atlantic Tunas* is an inter-government fishery organization responsible for the conservation of tunas and tuna-like species in the Atlantic Ocean and its adjacent seas.

ICW the *Intracoastal Waterway* extends over 2,400 miles along the Atlantic and Gulf coasts of the United States. As the name implies ("Intra" means within) it is a largely sheltered waterway within the coastline, making use of natural waterways such as bays, sounds, estuaries, and rivers, along with man-made canals. *ICW* aids-to-navigation can be differentiated from other navigational aids by the yellow logo (a triangle, square, or bar). *ICW* markers are red-right heading south or west. This puts the red aids-to-navigation on the mainland side of the *ICW*.

IHB the permanent secretariat for the IHO is the *International Hydrographic Bureau*. *See* IHO

IHO the *International Hydrographic Organization* has established standard forms, abbreviations, and symbols that are used throughout the world on nautical charts. Many of their recommendations have been adopted by the

United States for use on NOAA charts. *Chart No. 1*, which is not a chart but a booklet, defines the symbols and abbreviations that are used on nautical charts published in the United States. *See also* NOAA

IMO   the *International Meteorological Organization* was founded in 1873. Its international member countries pool their knowledge of meteorology and operational hydrology in the study of normal and episodic events. *See also* WHO

IMO   an abbreviation for the *International Maritime Organization*. The London-based IMO is a United Nations organization whose decisions have treaty status throughout most of the world. The IMO publishes the *International Regulations for Preventing Collisions at Sea* (IRPCS), which sets out the "Rules-of-the-Road" to be followed by all vessels at sea. *See also* GMDSS; SOLAS

IMR   an abbreviation for the *international measuring rule*. *See* IMS

IMS   the *International Measuring System* is a handicapping measuring system for cruising and racing yachts, managed by the ORC. *See also* ORC

In   a hydrographic abbreviation (not italicized) that is used in NOAA charts to indicate an *inlet*.

INMARSAT   an acronym for *International Marine Satellite*. It is an international telecommunications company founded in 1979, originally as an intergovernmental organization. It operates eleven (as of 2005) geosynchronous telecommunications satellites.

I/O an *Inboard/Outboard* is usually seen on mid-sized powerboats. The engine is mounted inboard, and the drive unit, which is similar to the bottom section of an outboard engine, is mounted outside the hull, usually on the transom. *See also* OB

IOR the *International Offshore Rule* is an international measurement rule for offshore racing yachts, originally adopted in 1970.

IPS Volvo-Penta's new, proprietary *inboard performance system* consists of an inboard engine, with an under-the-hull propulsion unit that can rotate for steering. It has two counter-rotating propellers in line with each other that are in *front* of the underwater unit, which includes the inboard engine's water intake and an underwater exhaust system.

IPX an IPX7 designation means that a GPS case can withstand accidental immersion in one meter of water for 30 minutes. An IPX8 designation is for continuous underwater use.

I Q or **I Qk** or **Int Qk** a non-italicized abbreviation used in NOAA charts to indicate *interrupted quick* (as in a flashing light).

IR *infrared* is a wavelength longer than that of visible light, but shorter than that of microwave radiation. Infrared transmitters are the common hand-held units used to remotely control electronic equipment.

IRC the *International Raceboard Class* rules are handicapping rating rules for racers/cruisers. They are co-produced in Britain and France and have been adopted all over the world. For years, U.S. race organizers resisted the idea of using these single-number rating rules, but now it seems the shift is toward their acceptance.

IRI an *infra-red illuminator* projects a beam of infra-red light, invisible to the naked eye, but which illuminates the scene received by a *night vision device*. See also NVD

IRPCS the *International Regulations for Preventing Collisions at Sea*. In the U.S. the abbreviation is COLREGS. See COLREGS

ISO and ISO-14001 (certification) the ISO is an *International Organization for Standardization*, and is a network of national standards institutes worldwide. The ISO standards are non-governmental and voluntary, adopted by companies desiring to improve their quality. ISO-14001 specifies the recommended standards for yacht manufacturers.

ISAF the *International Sailing Federation* is a world governing body for the sport. Its *racing rules of sailing* are revised and published every four years.

IYRS the *International Yacht Restoration School* teaches the skills, history, and art of restoring, maintaining, and building classic boats. Its staff and supporters share the mission of preserving our maritime heritage and working waterfronts.

IYRU the *International Yacht Racing Union* was founded in 1906. It establishes racing rules as well as building regulations for international sailboat classes, and overseas regattas. National sailing organizations, such as the *United States Yacht Racing Union* (USYRU) and the British *Royal*

Yachting Association (RYA) are affiliated with the IYRU. See also RYA; USYRU

J

J in sail measurement, "J" is the distance measured from the foreside of the mast to the point where the forestay attaches to the deck or bowsprit, in a direction level with the waterline.

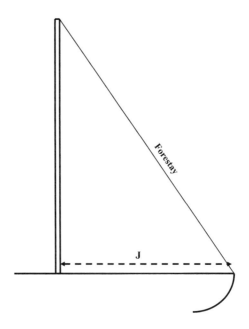

K

K an italicized hydrographic abbreviation used in NOAA charts to indicate that the seabed at that point has *kelp*.

kc an abbreviation for *kilocycles* (per second). This abbreviation has largely been replaced with the term *kilo-Hertz* (kHz). See Hz

kHz see Hz

KKK (alternators) these are heavy-duty alternators that meet the KKK-A-1822 federal standards for alternator characteristics, which includes the ability to operate continuously at full output in high temperatures, oversized bearings, heavy duty brushes, and heavy duty diodes.

Knot the mariner's unit of speed on the water which equals one *nautical mile per hour*. The *nautical mile* is the length of one minute of latitude, and the *international nautical mile* is 6076.1 feet. It is incorrect and redundant to refer to speed on the water as "knots per hour." See also NM.

kn or **kt** or **kts** the abbreviation for *knots*. See Knot.

L

L the abbreviation sometimes used for *latitude*, although *Lat* is more common. *L* is often used in problems where two or more *latitudes* are used. In those cases these *latitudes* are usually numbered with subscripts, such as L_1 and L_2. *See* LAT

L on meteorological weather charts indicates the center of a *low pressure system*.

λ the Greek letter *lambda*, is sometimes used to indicate longitude. *See* LON

LAN *local apparent noon* is the moment when the sun transits the observer's meridian. At this moment the sun is at its highest point in the sky for that day, and this is the only time when an uncompensated celestial observation will yield a line of latitude.

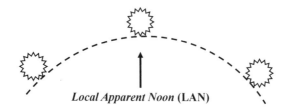

Local Apparent Noon (LAN)

LAT a commonly used abbreviation for *latitude*, although *L* or the Greek letter *phi*, (Φ) are occasionally used. *Latitude* is the arc distance of a point measured from the equator toward either pole, measured in degrees, North or

LEOLUT   61

South, from 0 degrees (at the equator) to 90 degrees (at the poles). *See* L

LAT   the abbreviation for *lowest astronomical tide*, a theoretical calculation of the influence of the moon and the sun that will create the most likely lowest tide level.

LAT   in celestial navigation an abbreviation for *local apparent time*.

LCD   the *liquid crystal display* is currently the leading flat-panel display technology which, on recreational boats, has largely replaced the cathode ray tube in LORANs, radars, and other graphic display units because of its low power requirements and small size. *Liquid crystals* change orientation under an applied electric field and can thereby block or pass light. The *thin film display* (TFD) is a similar type of display. *See also* TFD

LED   the *light emitting diode* is a solid-state, low voltage, low current, long life light that was originally only used for indicator lights in electronic equipment. Now, clusters of LEDs are used for navigation lights, trailer lights, cabin lights, and flashlights.

LEO   satellites that are operating at an altitude close to the surface of the earth are referred to as being in a *low earth orbit*, and consequently have orbital times of considerably less than 24 hours. *See also* eLED

LEOLUT   *see* LUT

LEOSAR the *Low Altitude Earth Orbit Search and Rescue* is a satellite system that is part of the COMPAS-SARSAT Search and Rescue system. The satellites orbit at an altitude of 528 miles, and circle the Earth every 100 minutes. These satellites receive distress signals from EPIRBs and determine their location using doppler. This information is then relayed to the *Rescue Coordination Center* (RCC) via the *local user terminal* (LUT)—a satellite ground station—and the *Mission Control Center* (MCC). *See also* COMPAS-SARSAT; LUT; MCC; RCC

LF in the electromagnetic spectrum, *low frequency* specifies frequencies between 30 and 300 kilohertz (kHz). *See* Hz

LIDAR an acronym for *light detection and ranging*. It is a sensing system that, in conjunction with GPS, can be used to map the bottom contours of a body of water. By measuring the round-trip travel time of a laser beam, depths can be calculated, provided that the water is clear enough.

Li-Ion an electric cell, or battery, that uses *lithium ion* technology. The Li-Ion battery is lighter than other batteries, less toxic for disposal, and has the longest operating times between recharges. Li-Ion batteries are more expensive than either NiCad or NiMH batteries. *See also* NiCad; NiMH

LL a common abbreviation for *latitude and longitude*. *See* LAT; LON

LLS in sail measurement the *luff length of the spinnaker* is the greatest length of the luff and leach, measured around the edges of the sail.

LOA 63

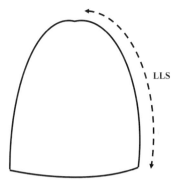

The measurement for the
Luff Length of a Spinnaker (LLS)

LMT just as GMT is the mean solar time measured at Greenwich, *Local Mean Time* is the mean solar time measured at any given local meridian. *See also* ZT (Zone Time)

LNB the Coast Guard's designation for *large navigational buoy*.

LNG *liquefied natural gas* is the term given to natural gas that is transported in large quantities, under high pressure, and low temperature.

LNM the Coast Guard's *Local Notice to Mariners*. It was once available by subscription via the Postal Service but since 2004, to improve service and reduce costs, it is now exclusively available via the Internet for each of the Coast Guard Districts.

LOA a boat's *length over all* is the entire length of a boat, including such bow and stern protuberances as a bowsprit and/or boomkin.

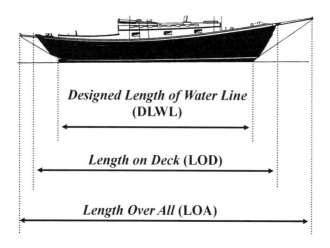

LOD *length on deck* is the length measured on deck from the bow to stern. This measurement is exclusive of extensions such as a bowsprit or boomkin.

LON an abbreviation for *longitude*, although sometimes *Lo* or the Greek letter lambda (λ), are also used. *Longitude* is the angular direction between the prime meridian at Greenwich, England and the meridian of a particular point.

LOP *line of position* is the imaginary line on which your boat is located. All navigational systems determine a vessel's position, or "fix," by the intersection of two or more LOPs. A LOP can be straight, circular, hyperbolic or, in the case of GPS, spherical.

LORAN an acronym for the *long range navigation* system that was introduced during World War II, and was then superseded by the improved *Loran-C*, which operates in the 100 kHz band. It is a land-based system that uses very high power transmitters operating at very low frequencies. Since its *lines of position* (LOPs) are hyperbolic, it is termed a hyperbolic navigation system. These hyperbolic lines are shown on some charts where "fixes" can be plotted directly—however many LORAN receivers, through the use of algorithms, provide latitude and longitude on a direct readout. LORAN has been largely replaced by GPS, but is still an operational navigation system. *See also* GPS

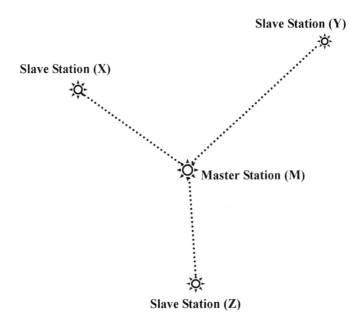

A Typical LORAN Chain

LP   in sail measurement, "LP" is the distance from the clew of the jib to the luff of the jib, measured to intersect the luff of the jib at a 90-degree angle.

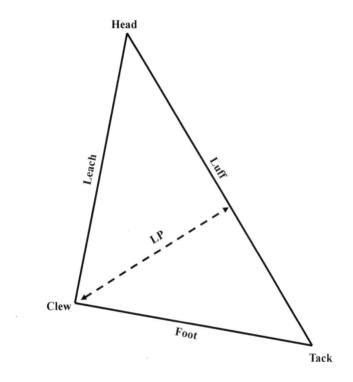

LPG *liquid petroleum gas* is one of the most commonly used and easily available galley-stove fuels, with a high BTU content; since it is heavier than air, special installation standards and equipment maintenance are necessary for safety.

LRAD an acronym for *long range acoustic device*, also sometimes referred to as a *sonic cannon*. LRAD is an acoustical dish used by the Navy that blasts a tight beam of siren-like sound over long distances, and is primarily used as a non-lethal deterrent to approaching small craft.

lrg an italicized hydrographic abbreviation used in NOAA charts to indicate *large*.

LS   a non-italicized abbreviation used in NOAA charts to indicate a *lightship*.

lt   an italicized hydrographic abbreviation used in NOAA charts to indicate a *light*.

LT HO or **Lt Ho**   a non-italicized abbreviation used in NOAA charts to indicate a *lighthouse*.

LUT   a *local user terminal* is a satellite ground station, used to receive distress signals from the COSPAS-SARSAT satellite system. There are two types of LUTs: LEOLUTs are designed to operate with the LEOSAR satellite constellation, and GEOLUTS are designed to operate with the GEOSAR satellite constellation. *See* COSPAS-SARSAT; EPIRB;

LWL   the *length of the waterline*. It is the length of the waterline on a vessel when the boat is floating upright. It is measured as a straight line from bow to stern, excluding any section of the rudder that may be at or above the water's surface. On displacement hulls, this length is tied in mathematically with the vessel's maximum practical speed. *See also* DLWL

LWOS   an abbreviation for *low water ordinary springs*, which is an average of the low water levels associated with spring tides, that is, those tides that occur when the Earth, Moon, and Sun are in line. *See also* MLLW; MLW; MLWS

M

M   an italicized hydrographic abbreviation used in NOAA charts to indicate that the seabed at that point is *mud*.

m   an italicized qualifying term used as a hydrographic abbreviation on NOAA charts meaning *medium*. It is used with the hydrographic abbreviation S, for *sand*, to indicate the size of the sand particles. (i.e. *mS*).

m   an abbreviation for *meter*, the basic unit of measurement in the metric system, which was first established in 1795. In the *foot-pound-second* (f.p.s.) system, this is equivalent to 39.37 inches.

mA or **ma**   the abbreviation for *milliamps*, or *milliamperes*. It is 1/1000 of an ampere. *See A*

MAFMC   the *Mid-Atlantic Fishery Management Council* is responsible for the management of fisheries in federal waters off the Mid-Atlantic States.

MARPA   *mini automatic radar plotting* is a target tracking system that is now a part of nearly all color radars. It is a way of tracking multiple targets that you designate, and provides the courses, speeds, and bearing distances of these targets.

MARPOL   the *International Convention for the Prevention of Pollution from Ships*, (better known as MARPOL), is one of the most important international agreements on the subject of marine pollution. In 1988 a Federal law went into effect for all of the U.S. waters, prohibiting discharging plastics, paper, garbage, glass, metal, or food wastes into these waters. The MARPOL international treaty also requires a *trash placard* on boats 26 feet or over in length. This *trash placard* briefly explains the MARPOL regulations. In addition, boats 40 feet and over in length are required to also display a written trash-disposal plan.

mb   the millibar is a unit for expressing atmospheric pressure. Sea level pressure is normally close to 1013 mb.

mb   the abbreviation for *megabyte*.

MCA   the MCA is a code of standards promulgated by the British Maritime and Coastguard Agency for large charter vessels.

MCA   an abbreviation for the *marine cranking amps* of a battery. It is the number of amps a 12-volt battery can deliver for 30 seconds at 32° F. while maintaining its voltage above 7.2 volts. See also CCA

MCC   *Mission Control Centers* have been set up around the world to process Search and Rescue data from the COSPAS-SARSAT satellite system. That information is then sent to the appropriate *Rescue Coordination Centers* (RCC). See COSPAS-SARSAT; LUT; RCC

MCO   *see* MSO

Medevac   the Coast Guard's abbreviation for *medical evacuation*.

MEK   an abbreviation for *methyl ethyl ketone*, a solvent for polyester and vinylester resins.

MEKP an abbreviation for *methyl ethyl ketone peroxide*, a liquid catalyst added to polyester resins and vinylester resins. As the catalyst mixes with the resin, a chemical reaction occurs, creating heat which cures (hardens) the resin.

MF in the electromagnetic spectrum *medium frequency* designates the frequencies between 300 kilohertz (kHz) and 3 megahertz (MHz). *See also* Hz

MFCMA the *Magnuson Fishery Conservation and Management Act* of 1980 established the 200-mile fishery conservation zone and regional fishery management council. It has since been renamed the *Magnuson-Stevens Fishery Conservation and Management Act* (MSFCMA).

MFD a *multi-function display* has the ability to display the outputs of more than one piece of navigation gear (i.e. chart plotter, radar, depth-sounder, etc.) on a single screen.

MHHW *mean higher high water* is the high water level to which all bridge clearances are referenced and charted. In most parts of the world (except for a few places such as portions of the Gulf of Mexico) there are two high and two low tides each day. The Moon is the primary influence on the tides, and since the Moon's orbital plane around the Earth is canted in relation to the equator, one of the two daily highs is higher than the other. If we take the average, or mean, of only the higher of the two daily highs over a period of 19 years, we have the *mean higher high water*. (Note: The 19-year period is called a *tidal epoch*, during which time every possible combination of the positions of the Earth, Sun, and Moon occurs, before the *tidal epoch* is repeated).

MHWS 71

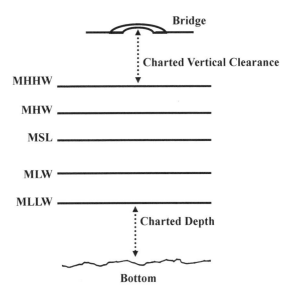

MHW *mean high water* is the mean or average of high waters over a period of 19 years ast a particular location. *See also* MHHW

MHWS *mean high water springs* is the average of the high water levels during spring tides over a period of 19 years. *See also* MHHW

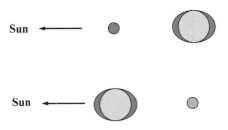

Spring Tides occur when the Sun, Earth, and Moon are in line

MHz *see Hz*

MI an italicized hydrographic abbreviation used in NOAA charts to indicate that the seabed at that point is *marl*.

MLB the Coast Guard's abbreviation for *motor lifeboat*.

MLLW *mean lower low water*. If we take the average, or mean, of only the lower of the two daily lows over a period of 19 years, we have the *mean lower low water*. The term *mean lower low water* is frequently used in NOAA weather forecasts, and in the U.S. it is used as the reference for depth soundings on charts.

MLW *mean low water* is the average level of low tides that occur in a specific location over a 19-year period of time. *See also* MLLW

MLWS *mean low water springs* is the mean, or average, of low water levels during spring tides over a 19-year period.. *See also* MLLW

mm the abbreviation for *millimeter*, a thousandth of a meter.

MMC the *multi-media card* offers the capability to record, store, review, and recall electronic data and displays on equipment designed for its use.

MMPA the *Marine Mammal Protection Act*, which was passed by Congress in 1972, prohibits, with certain exceptions, the taking of marine mammals in U.S. waters and by U.S. citizens on the high seas, and the transportation of marine mammals and marine mammal products into the U.S.

MMSI   the *Maritime Mobile Service Identification Number* is used in conjunction with DSC and AIS on the VHF-FM marine band. *See* AIS; DSC; VHF-FM

Mo   an abbreviation used in NOAA charts to indicate a *morse code* light, fog signal, or radio transmission.

MOB   an abbreviation for *Man Overboard*. *See also* COB

MOM   the *man overboard module* is an important item in the recovery of a person overboard. It consists of a canister, which is located on the stern of the boat; when activated and deployed, the canister has an inflatable horseshoe buoyancy device capable of supporting a 250 lb. person; an inflatable locator pylon which reaches 6 feet above the water with a steady-state light on top; and a self-deploying 16-inch sea anchor.

MORC   the *Midget Ocean Racing Club* was founded in 1954 and runs offshore races for sailboats under 30-feet overall length. It is the objective of the MORC measurement rule to allow different types of boats to be rated, handicapped, and raced fairly.

MOSFET   an acronym for *metal oxide semiconductor field effect transistor*. It is the most common field-effect transistor used in both digital and analog circuits.

MPA   a *marine protection area* is a specific geographic area where certain types of human activity have been curtailed.

This may include fishing restrictions, anchoring that may lead to the destruction of the seabed, etc.

mph   *miles per hour*, and = Knots x .868.

MPI   *multi-port* (fuel) *injection*, or *multi-point* (fuel) *injection* provides significant advantages over the traditional carburetor in internal combustion engines.

MPOSS   the Coast Guard's abbreviation for a *multi-purpose oil skimming system*.

MRAA   the *Marine Retailer's Association of America* was founded in 1971 as a non-profit organization for the purpose of giving a voice to marine dealers throughout the United States.

MRFSS   since 1979 the *Marine Recreational Fishery Statistics Survey* has provided a database for estimating the impact of recreational fishing on the nation's resources by calculating how many people are fishing and how many fish they are taking.

MSA   the *Magnuson-Stevens Act* is an abbreviated title for the *Magnuson-Stevens Fishery Conservation and Management Act*. See MSFCMA

MSAS   the *Multifunctional Transport Satellite-based Augmentation System* is used throughout Asia to provide satellite navigational corrections that improves accuracy. The MSAS is similar to the U.S. WAAS system.

MSD   in the 1970s the federal government made it illegal for boats to discharge untreated sewage into the waters of

MTBE 75

the U.S., including up to three miles offshore along the coasts, unless that effluent has been treated by an approved *marine sanitation device* (MSD). States also have the option of declaring sensitive waters as *no discharge zones* (NDZ), where no discharge is allowed, including that of approved MSDs. Boats in these areas must use a holding tank. *See also* NDZ

MSFCMA the *Magnuson Fishery Conservation and Management Act* of 1980 (MFCMA) established the 200-mile fishery conservation zone and regional fishery management council. It has since been renamed the *Magnuson-Stevens Fishery Conservation and Management Act* (MSFCMA).

MSL *mean sea level* is usually a designation used in areas where there is no appreciable tidal range.

MSO the *manufacturer's statement of origin* is also known as the *manufacturer's certificate of origin* (MCO), and contains the boat's HIN and engine serial number(s)—if applicable. It shows when the boat was built and transferred to the retail dealer for resale purposes or directly to the customer. The MSO is necessary when you register or document the boat, or apply for insurance. It will be transferred to the lender if the boat is financed. The MSO should be included in the papers received at the time of purchase.

MSO the Coast Guard's abbreviation for *Marine Safety Office*.

MTBE *methyl tertiary butyl ether* is a chemical compound which contains oxygen and was added to *reformulated*

gasoline, or *oxygenate gasoline*, to boost its octane or to meet clean fuel oxygen requirements. But in response to concerns of traces of MTBE in the drinking water supply, reports that it was making motorists sick, and that it was causing deterioration in fiberglass fuel tanks, many states banned its use and the EPA has finally dropped its oxygenated fuel requirement effective May 2006. *See* RFG

M/V or **MV** a prefix placed before the name of a ship to indicate that she is a *motor vessel*.

MVT an abbreviation for *multi-vision technology*. *See* MFD

N

N *north* is a cardinal direction to which any other angular measurement is referenced. It is represented either as 0 degrees or 360 degrees, and may be either Compass, Magnetic, or True *North*. *See also* Var

NA an abbreviation for *not available*.

NAD the *National American Datum*, also known as the geodetic datum, is the mapping of the continent using astronomical data, an assumed underlining ellipsoid, and clever mathematics, to establish a latitude and longitude grid. The 1927 model (before satellite mapping) was known as NAD-27, and was the first of these models, later supplemented by NAD-83. *See also* CD; WGS; WGS-84; NAD-83

NAVTEX 77

NAD-83   on current U.S. charts the horizontal reference *Datum* is the *North American Datum of 1983* (NAD 83) which is considered to be the equivalent of the *World Geodetic System* 1984 (WGS 84). This is the default *Datum* setting for most GPS receivers sold in the U.S. *See also* CD; NAD; WGS; WGS-84

NAEBM   in 1979 the *National Association of Engine and Boat Manufacturers* (NAEBM) merged with the *Boating Industry Association of Chicago* (BIA) to form the *National Marine Manufacturer's Association* (NMMA). *See* NMMA

NAMS   the *National Association of Marine Surveyors* is an organization which, since 1962, has been composed of marine surveyor professionals. It was originally named the *Yacht Safety Bureau* until its reorganization.

NASBLA   the *National Association of Boating Law Administrators* is an organization representing the boating authorities of all 50 states and U.S. territories. It works toward safe boating and a uniformity of boating laws in all the states.

NAVSAT   NAVSAT is a satellite navigation system that is based on the receiver's ability to measure doppler shift from orbiting satellites. The system is primarily used aboard large ships and naval vessels.

NAVSTAR   the *NAVSTAR Global Positioning System*. *See* GPS

NAVTEX   the NAVTEX is used for the broadcast of localized *Maritime Safety Information* (MSI), using radio *Telex*. The system mainly operates in medium frequencies with a normal range of about 300 nautical miles. The NAVTEX receiver is a compact unit with integral printer, display, and a keyboard that allows selection of the appropriate station and subject matter. Once programmed, the unit can operate unattended, with messages received and printed-out automatically.

NAYRU   *see* USYRU

NBSAC   the *National Boating Safety Advisory Council* was established by the Federal Boating Safety Act of 1971, and is an advisory council to the Coast Guard and Secretary of Homeland Security regarding boating safety matters.

N by E   *North by East* is a compass direction. *N by E* equals 11.25 degrees or 11 degrees 15 minutes. *See also* Var

N by W   *North by West* is a compass direction. *N by W* equals 348.75 degrees or 348 degrees 45 minutes. *See* NNE for an illustration of the 32-point Compass Rose. *See also* Var

NDZ   a *no discharge zone*. *See also* MSD

NE   *North East* is an intercardinal direction, or 45 degrees. It may be referenced either to Compass, Magnetic, or true North. *See also* Var

NE by E   *North East by East* is a compass direction. *NE by E* equals 56.25 degrees or 56 degrees 15 minutes. *See also* Var

NE by N   *North East by North* is a compass direction. *NE by N* equals 33.75 degrees or 33 degrees 45 minutes. It may be referenced either to Compass, Magnetic, or True North. *See also* Var

Negres   the Coast Guard's abbreviation for *Negative Results*, *No*, or *None*.

NEMFC   the *New England Fishery Management Council* is one of eight regional councils established by the MFCMA. It manages fishery resources within the federal 200 mile limit off the coasts of Maine, New Hampshire, Rhode Island, and Connecticut. *See also* MFCMA

NEXRAD   NEXRAD and its agencies was established in 1988 to provide radar displays from its 158 weather radar stations.

NFPA   the *National Fire Protection Association* is an international, nonprofit organization whose codes cover many aspects of flammable materials, both on land and at sea.

NGA   the *National Geospatial-Intelligence Agency* was known as the *National Imagery and Mapping Agency* (NIMA) before 2004. The NIMA was established October 1, 1996 to centralize responsibility for imagery and mapping using digital processing technology. The creation of the NIMA brought together the *Defense Mapping Agency* (DMA), the *Central Imaging Office* (CIO), and the *Defense Dissemination Program Office* (DDPO). NGA's Maritime Safety Information page lists many publications that are available on-line at no charge, including *Bowditch*, light lists, Notice to Mariners, sight-reduction tables for celestial navigation, weather, currents, harbor entries, and much more.

NGS   NOAA's *National Geodetic Survey* was formerly the *U.S. Coast and Geodetic Survey*. NGS defines and manages a national coordinate system. This network, the *National Spatial Reference System* (NSRS), provides the foundation for transportation and communication; mapping and charting; and a multitude of scientific and engineering applications.

Ni-Cad   an abbreviation for a *nickel-cadmium* rechargeable cell, or battery. *See also* Li-Ion; NiMH

NIMA   *see* NGA

NiMH   an abbreviation for *nickel-metal hydrid* cells or batteries. Unlike NiCad batteries, NiMH batteries do not use heavy metals that are environmentally toxic. They also can store up to 50% more power than NiCad batteries and do not suffer memory effects. *See also* Li-Ion; NiCad; NiMH

NIMA   an acronym for the *National Imaging and Mapping Agency*, which is the distributor of topographic maps as part of the Department of the Interior.

NM   the *nautical mile* is the length of one minute of latitude. The *international nautical mile* is 6076.1 feet. There are approximately 1.15 statute miles in a nautical mile. The *nautical mile* is used to designate distance at sea and is the measurement used on most charts. The *statute mile*, which is 5280 feet, is used on some charts of the United States' inland waters, such as the *Intracoastal Waterway* and the *Great Lakes*.

NM   an abbreviation for *Notice to Mariners*. *See* LNM

NMBA   members of the *National Marine Bankers Association* provide financing to the marine industry in a variety of ways. Some offer loans directly to customers for boat purchases or refinancing, while others provide financing through dealers. Commercial lenders also finance new and used inventory for dealers of boats and motors.

NMDMP   the *National Marine Debris Monitoring Program*, whose volunteer members conduct monthly beach cleanups and debris surveys at selected sites along the U.S. coastline.

NMEA   the *National Marine Electronics Association* is the unifying force behind the entire marine electronics industry, and is the organization that promotes and promulgates standards for marine electronics.

NMEA 0183   this has been an international standard for interfacing electronic equipment on board for many years. It defines the electronic signal requirements, data transmission, protocol and time, and specific sentence formats for a 4800-baud serial data bus. Each bus may have one talker and multiple listeners. The newer *NMEA 2000* has many advantages. *See* NMEA 2000

NMEA 2000   this is a standard containing the standards of a serial-data network to inter-connect marine electronics equipment designed for this standard. It is multi-master and self configuring, with no network controller. Equipment designed to this standard has the ability to share data, including commands and status. *See* NMEA 0183

NMFC   an abbreviation for the *National Marine Fisheries Council*. *See* NMFS

NMFS   the *National Marine Fisheries Service* is an agency of the U.S. Department of Commerce. The *NOAA Fisheries Service* acts as a steward to conserve, protect, and manage living marine resources in a way that ensures their continuation and functioning as components of marine ecosystems, as well as affording economic opportunities.

nmiles   an abbreviation for *nautical miles. See* NM

NMMA   the members of the *National Marine Manufacturer's Association* consists of more than 1,400 companies that produce products for recreational boating. It was formed in 1979 as a non-profit association, whose roots go back to 1904 when the *National Association of Engine and Boat Manufacturers* (NAEBM) was founded. *See also* NAEBM

NNE   *North North East* is a compass direction. *NNEE* equals 22.40 degrees or 22 degrees 30 minutes. *See also* Var

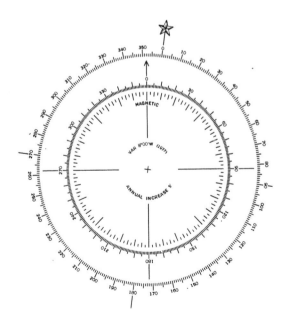

NNW *North North West* is a compass direction. *NNW* equals 337.50 degrees or 337 degrees 30 minutes. *See also* Var

NOAA the *National Oceanic and Atmospheric Administration* was formed in 1970, when several government agencies came together to establish the agency responsible for marine weather forecasts, nautical charts (through the NOS), and the Search and Rescue satellite program, among many other services.

NOAA Fisheries Service *see* NMFS

NOOD the *National Offshore One Design* regattas are held throughout the United States and Canada for sailboats in the *One Design* category.

NORAD although not directly related to the recreational boater, this is vital to the security of all Americans and Canadians. The *North American Aerospace Defense Command* uses ground-based radar, airborne radar, satellites, fighter aircraft, proven command structures and intelligence capabilities to enforce control of the skies over the United States and Canada.

NOS the *National Ocean Survey* prepares most of the charts for U.S. waters, with the exception of some charts prepared by the *Army Corps of Engineers*, such as those of the Mississippi, Ohio, and Tennessee rivers and their tributaries.

NOx *nitrogen oxides* are an unwanted emission from internal combustion engines. Current regulations prescribe the maximum amount of these emissions (as of 2005) and it's probable that stricter regulations in the near future will require the use of catalytic converters in the exhaust systems to meet those new standards. The catalytic converter, a honeycomb of ceramic coated with platinum, rhodium, or palladium, breaks down the NOx into *nitrogen* and *oxygen*. Engines so-equipped will have to have sophisticated diagnostics, adding expense and complexity. In addition, the catalytic converter runs extremely hot, creating a safety issue in a confined engine compartment.

NP RS-X   *see* RS-X

NSBC   the *National Safe Boating Council, Inc.* was organized in 1958 as a non-profit organization under the name *National Safe Boating Committee*. The goal of its diverse U.S. and Canadian membership is the advancement and promotion of safer boating through education.

NSHOF   the *National Sailing Hall of Fame & Museum* project was established on December 21, 2005. The Hall of Fame and sailing museum will find a home in Annapolis, MD as a non-profit educational institution dedicated to preserving the history and sport of sailing, and to honor those who have made outstanding contributions to that sport.

NSRS   the *National Spatial Reference System* (NSRS) provides the foundation for transportation and communication; mapping and charting; and a multitude of scientific and engineering applications.

Nt M   an alternative abbreviation for *nautical mile*. *See* NM

NVD   a *night vision device* can be either first, second or third generation technology, referenced to the type of light intensifier tube used. The higher the generation, the brighter and sharper is the received image. *See also* IRI

NW   an intercardinal direction, *North West*, or 315 degrees. It may be referenced either to Compass, Magnetic, or True North. *See also* Var

NW by N   *North West by North* is a compass direction. *NW by N* equals 326.25 degrees or 326 degrees 15 minutes. *See also* Var

NW by W   *North West by West* is a compass direction. *NW by W* equals 303.75 degrees or 303 degrees 45 minutes. *See also* Var

NWS   the *National Weather Service* provides mariners with high seas, coastal, and offshore forecasts; special marine warnings; marine weather statements; and Great Lakes forecasts.

NYYC   the *New York Yacht Club* opened their first clubhouse in Hoboken, NJ, across the Hudson River from Manhattan, in 1845. Two days later they began their annual tradition, the club's Regatta, that has continued for over 150 years.

O

OAN the *Ocean Action Network* is composed of grassroots activists.

OB an abbreviation for a detachable motor, the *outboard motor*, which is usually mounted on the transom (*outboard* of the hull) or sometimes installed in a motor-well inside the hull.

O/B a Coast Guard abbreviation denoting *on board*.

Obstn or **Obstr** an abbreviation used in NOAA charts to indicate an *obstruction*.

OC it is the mission of the *Ocean Conservancy* to provide a comprehensive and centralized source of ocean news, education, and conservation information.

Oc or **Occ** an abbreviation used in NOAA charts to indicate an *intermittent* or *occulting light*.

OCS the *Office of Coast Survey* is the oldest scientific organization in the United States, and since 1970 has been part the *National Oceanic and Atmospheric Administration's* (NOAA's) *National Ocean Service*. It is responsible for nautical chart data, collecting hydrographic data, and information programs, as well as for producing nautical charts for U.S. waters, its possessions, and territories. The origin of the OCS dates back to the days of Thomas Jefferson.

OEM an abbreviation for *original equipment manufacturer*. Thus, *OEM-approved* indicates that a manufacturer approves the use of that product in their equipment.

OMC the *Outboard Marine Corporation* is a company which has been around for many decades. It produces Evinrude and Johnson outboard motors, Stratos and Javelin bass-boats, Chris-Craft, and other pleasure boats. It recently filed for Chapter-11 bankruptcy.

OMEGA OMEGA was one of the early electronic navigation systems. It was originated by the United States and was also used by partner nations. Operation of the OMEGA system was terminated permanently in 1997 when GPS navigation became more practical. *See* GPS; Loran

Ω the Greek letter *Omega* (the last letter of the Greek alphabet) is often used as an abbreviation for *ohm(s)*, the unit of electrical resistance.

OOADP the *Open Ocean Aquatic Demonstration Project* was founded in 1998 as an aquaculture program for the waters between 3 and 200 miles offshore.

OPA-90 the *Oil Pollution Act of 1990* streamlined and strengthened the EPA's ability to respond to catastrophic oil spills.

OPD in February 1998 an *overfill protection device* was mandated for all propane tanks in the United States to prevent overfilling.

or an italicized hydrographic abbreviation used in NOAA charts to indicate *orange*.

ORBCOMM an acronym for the oldest of several satellite data communications companies that provides a global wireless data and a messaging system using *low earth orbit* (LEO) satellites. It provides a service similar to two-way paging or e-mail and is capable of sending alphanumeric data anywhere in the world.

ORC the *Offshore Racing Conference*, is recognized by the International Sailing Federation (ISAF), and was established to regulate international yacht racing. *See* ISAF

ORMA an acronym for the *Open Multihull Racing Association*.

OSTAR the *Single-handed Transatlantic Race* has been held every four years since 1960. Originally known as the OSTAR, *Observer Single-Handed Transatlantic Race*, the event has changed names twice, but still remains a single-handed Atlantic race. The course, depending on the route chosen, varies from about 2,800 miles (the direct route) to the longer route, via the Azores. The start is still from Plymouth, England as usual, but the finish line has been moved from New York to Newport, Rhode Island, for the second time.

OVHD PWR CAB an abbreviation used in NOAA charts to indicate an *overhead power cable*.

Oz an italicized hydrographic abbreviation used in NOAA charts to indicate that the seabed at that point is *ooze*.

P

P in sail measurement, "P" is the length of the luff of the mainsail. For ketches and yawls the length of the luff of the mizzen sail is designated as *Py*.

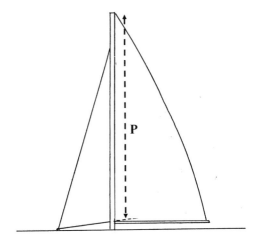

P an italicized hydrographic abbreviation used in NOAA charts to indicate that the seabed at that point is *pebbles*.

PA an abbreviation used in NOAA charts to indicate *position approximate*.

PBO *poly-para-phnylene-26 benzo*-biosoxazole, or *polybenzoxazole* for short, is a synthetic, expensive, high-strength line, used primarily for running-rigging. It is the strongest of the high-strength synthetic fibers, yet is lighter than the next-strongest, *HMPE*. *See* HMPE

PC   a naval architect's abbreviation for *prismatic coefficient*. CP and Cp are also used for this designation. *See* CP

P/C   the Coast Guard's abbreviation for *pleasure craft*.

PCB   an electronic *printed circuit board*.

PD   an abbreviation used in NOAA charts to indicate *position doubtful*.

PDM   the *power distribution module* distributes a single electrical power input to multiple individual outputs. Each of these outputs is protected from disabling the other outputs, and there are automatic resets when an individual output is interrupted due to an overload.

PFD   in the U.S. this is a abbreviation for a *personal flotation device*, in other words, a Coast Guard approved cushion or life jacket designed to keep a person afloat. Various categories of PFDs are available for varying conditions, circumstances, and body sizes. There are specific boat-equipment requirements for PFDs from the Coast Guard as well as from the individual states.

PFDMA   the *Personal Flotation Device Manufacturer's Association* is a membership organization that is a proponent for wearing PFDs on board. They are also active in hosting workshops, and providing educational material on PFDs.

PFMC   the *Pacific Fishery Management Council* is one of eight regional fishery management councils established by the Magnuson Fishery Conservation and Management Act of 1976 for the purpose of managing fisheries 3 to 200 miles offshore of the U.S. coastline. The PFMC is responsible for fisheries off California, Oregon, and Washington.

PH *performance handicap.* See PHRF

Φ the Greek letter Phi, is sometimes used to indicate Latitude. *See* LAT

PHRF *performance handicap racing fleet* is a system used to handicap racing and cruising type of sailboats by observed racing performance. PHRF (unlike IOR, MORC, IMS, or MHS) does not use measurements to calculate the standard speed of a boat, but does take measurements to identify any differences from what is considered standard.

PIW the Coast Guard's abbreviation for *person in the water.*

PLB the *personal locator beacon.* The PLB is a personal EPIRB that is usually attached to an individual and transmits an emergency signal which identifies that individual, rather than the boat. *See* EPIRB

Pnt the Coast Guard's abbreviation for *patient.*

POB the USCG abbreviation for *person(s) on board.*

PORTS the *Physical Oceanographic Real-Time System* is a NOAA program that includes centralized data acquisition and dissemination systems providing real-time water levels, currents, and other oceanographic and meteorological data from bays and harbors that can be accessed in a variety of user-friendly formats.

PPI in naval architecture *pounds per inch immersion*, is the amount of weight that would have to be added (or removed) to have a particular hull submerge (or raise) the waterline one inch.

PPI on radar displays, the *plan position indicator*, or the vessel's position at the center of the screen. For this reason a radar's screen is often called a *PPI Scope*. See Radar

Priv or **Priv maintd** an abbreviation used in NOAA charts to indicate *privately maintained* aids to navigation.

PVC an abbreviation for the thermoplastic *poly vinyl chloride*. It is a common synthetic material in use in the marine environment due to its resistance to weathering, water, and many chemicals. It is often the waterproofing material used for foulweather gear.

PWC *personal water craft* is the generic term for a group of small, water-jet-powered recreational boats manufactured and marketed under many proprietary names.

Py *see* P

Q

Q or **Qk Fl** an abbreviation used in NOAA charts to indicate a *quick flashing light*.

R

R an italicized hydrographic abbreviation used in NOAA charts to indicate that the seabed at that point is *rock* or *rocky*. *Rk* or *rky* are also sometimes used.

RACON a *radar transponder beacon*, or a *radio beacon*, or a *radio responder* responds to a received radar pulse by transmitting an identifiable Morse-encoded response back to the radar set on that set's frequency. This information is displayed on the radar screen along with the position of the *racon*. *Racons* and their identifying marks are usually indicated on charts and are used to identify aids to navigation, coastline positions, navigable spans under bridges, offshore platforms, and to warn of environmentally sensitive areas. See RADAR; R Bn

Radar an acronym for *radio detecting and ranging*. A marine radar is used to determine the distances and azimuths of land-masses, boats, and buoys by measuring the time between the transmission and return of an electromagnetic microwave signal which has been transmitted and reflected back from the *target*. In some cases this return signal may also be retransmitted by a *transponder* on the target, which is triggered by the original signal. See also RACON; RTE; SART

RAM as related to VHF-FM radios, this is an abbreviation for *remote access microphone*. This feature allows control of all of the functions of a cabin-installed VHF-FM radio, from the cockpit.

RBFF the *Recreational Boating and Fishing Foundation* is a non-profit organization that was established in 1998 to increase participation in recreational fishing and boating and to complement the ongoing conservation efforts of government agencies.

RBHB an abbreviation used in NOAA charts to indicate *red and black horizontal bands*.

R Bn or **Ro Bn** an abbreviation used in NOAA charts to indicate a *radio beacon*.

RCC the *Rescue Coordination Center* provides management and coordination of *Search and Rescue* (SAR) efforts by linking information received from the COSPAS-SARSAT satellite system, which detects distress signals, to a digital chart of the world that gives the precise location of the distress signal. *See also* COSPAS-SARSAT; LUT; MCC

RCDS the *Raster chart display systems* are computer-based navigation systems which are exact reproductions of the paper chart, and which use *Raster nautical charts* (RNC) and electronic positioning to provide an integrated navigational tool. The national hydrographic offices, such as the *Office of Coast Survey* (OCS) are producing RNCs and endorsing the use of RCDS. *See also* IHO; OCS; RNC

RCS *radar cross section* describes the reflectivity of a radar reflector. This reflectivity goes up by the fourth power of its radius for any given radar reflector.

rd an italicized hydrographic abbreviation used in NOAA charts to indicate *red*.

RDF   the *radio direction finder* was one of the first electronic navigation systems. It provides directions to radio transmitters, allowing lines of position to be plotted to determine a vessel's position.

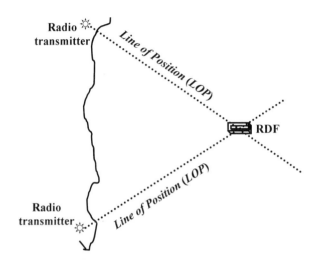

RECON   an organization whose volunteer divers collect information about coral reef environments, the health of those reefs, their key organisms, and any obvious human-induced impacts so that these coral reefs can be better preserved and protected. *See also* TDS Recon

RFG   *reformulated gasoline* is a gasoline with a different composition from regular gasoline, and has a lower aromatic content. It is blended to burn cleaner and reduce smog-forming and toxic pollutants in the air. The *Clean Air Act* requires that RFG be used in certain urban areas.

Rep or **rep**   an abbreviation used in NOAA charts to indicate *reported*.

Restr   an abbreviation used in NOAA charts to indicate *restricted*.

Rf   an abbreviation used in NOAA charts to indicate *reef*.

rf or **RF**   *radio frequency* or *radio frequencies* is that portion of the electromagnetic spectrum between *audio frequencies* (af) and infrared, and is used to transmit and receive radio signals.

RF   an abbreviation for a *range finder*, which determines the distance of an object from the observer using optics, sonar, radar, or laser.

RFA   the *Recreational Fishing Alliance* is a national grassroots political action organization representing individual sport fishermen and the sport fishing industry. The RFA mission is to safeguard the rights of saltwater anglers, protect marine, boat, and tackle industry jobs, and insure the long-term sustainability of U.S. saltwater fisheries.

RFI or **RFI/EMI**   RFI is an abbreviation for *radio frequency interference* and EMI is an abbreviation for *electromagnetic interference*. EMI and RFI are interferences emitted by electrical devices that cause other electronic devices to malfunction. Many countries have legislation and standards to govern and minimize these unwanted and interfering emissions.

Rge   an abbreviation used in NOAA charts to indicate the on-land aids to navigation, *ranges*.

RIB   a *ridged inflatable boat* is an inflatable boat with a ridged bottom, usually fiberglass or aluminum, which enables the boat to get up on a plane easily for high speed travel, and protects the bottom from debris in the water or when being beached. The downside of a RIB is that it cannot be folded up like a normal inflatable for compact storage, however the inflatable section can be collapsed into the ridged hull.

RINA   RINA certification indicates a yacht has met the requirements and specifications for design, engineering, construction, testing, and documentation associated with the RINA certification process, by the International Standards Organization.

Rk   see R

Rky   see R

R Lt   an abbreviation used in NOAA charts to indicate a *red light*.

R MAST   an abbreviation used in NOAA charts to indicate a *radio mast* (or Radio Tower).

RNC   *see* RCDS

R/O   an abbreviation for *reverse osmosis*. In *reverse osmosis* an osmotic membrane is used as an extremely fine filter to create drinking water from salty or contaminated water. The name derives from the operation of putting the salt water on one side of the membrane and applying great pressure in order to stop, and then reverse, the normal osmotic process. R/O units are used on boats to create fresh water, and have seen substantial improvements in recent years.

RORC   the *Royal Ocean Racing Club*, founded in 1925, organizes a full domestic UK racing season, as well as the Rolex Fastnet Race and the Rolex Commodores' Cup.

ROV   the *remotely operated vehicle* is usually a small, robotic submarine with television capabilities, used to explore the sea bottom.

RPS   *range of positive stability* is the capsize angle of a boat, or the angle beyond which a boat will not right itself, but continue to roll to a 180-degree capsize. *See also* Gz

RPS or **rps**   an abbreviation for *revolutions per second*.

RS-X or **NP RS-X**   the proprietary name for the NeilPryde Company's Olympic Class windsurfers. The windsurfer board and rig are built to ISAF one design standards. *See also* ISAF

RTCM   the *Radio Technical Committee for Maritime Service*. In the United States the Federal Communications Commission and U.S. Coast Guard use RTCM standards to specify radar systems, EPIRBs, and DSC (Digital Selective Calling).

RTE   a *radar target enhancer* is simply a radar reflector.

Ru   an abbreviation used in NOAA charts to indicate *ruins*.

RWVS   an abbreviation used in NOAA charts to indicate *red and white vertical stripes*.

RYA the *Royal Yachting Association*, formerly the *Yacht Racing Association*, was founded in 1875 in the United Kingdom. It is involved with all phases of yachting, sailing, and powerboat interests. *See also* IYRU

S

S *South* is one of the cardinal directional points. It is represented as 180 degrees, and may be referenced either to Compass, Magnetic, or True *North*. *See also* Var

S an italicized hydrographic abbreviation used in NOAA charts to indicate that the seabed at that point is *sand*.

SA *selective availability* was an error that was deliberately introduced into the civilian and commercial GPS system by the Department of Defense for national security. *Selective availability* was discontinued, by Presidential order, in 2000. *See* DGPS; GPS

SAE the *Society of Automotive Engineers* is composed of engineers, business executives, educators, and students from over 97 countries who share information and standards development, and exchange ideas for advancing the engineering of mobility systems on both land and sea. Many of the safety standards they recommend are incorporated in the ABYC's publication *Safety Standards for Small Craft*. *See also* ABYC

SAME *special area message encoding* is an alert signal that is included in VHF-FM marine weather channel broadcasts which will trigger an alarm on SAME-equipped weather receivers. This alerts the user to potential severe weather conditions in the listener's immediate area.

SAMS the *Society of Accredited Marine Surveyors* is an organization of marine surveyors who have accumulated time in the profession, have proven technical skills, and are expected to follow a course of continued education to maintain their accreditation.

SAR *search and rescue*, which can be provided by either governmental or private agencies.

SARSAT *see* COMPAS-SARSAT

SART an acronym for *search and rescue transponder*. SARTs respond to a search vessel's radar beam with a series of blips that show up strongly on the screen. A SART will not send a distress signal to a satellite, like an EPIRB, but acts to guide a rescuing vessel to the location of the boat or life raft in trouble. *See also* RADAR

SAS an abbreviation for *safety at sea*.

SBIP an abbreviation for *super boat international productions*, an organization that manages offshore powerboat racing, among other duties. In January 2005 they combined their resources with the *American Powerboat Association* (APBA) to promote the sport of offshore powerboat racing. The new organization, *World Powerboat Racing, Inc.* (WPR) has a ten year licensing

SE by E

agreement with the *American Powerboat Racing Association*. *See also* APBA; WPR

S by E   *South by East* is a compass direction. *S by E* equals 168.75 degrees or 168 degrees 45 minutes. *See also* Var

S by W   *South by West* is a compass direction. *S by W* equals 191.25 degrees or 191 degrees 15 minutes. It may be referenced either to Compass, Magnetic, or True North. *See also* Var

SCRIMP   the *seeman composites resin infusion molding process* is the state-of-the-art hull and deck vacuum-assisted resin transfer molding method used for creating decks and hulls. The SCRIMP composite sandwich consists of a biaxial/unidirectional inner skin, with a biaxial Kevlar/E-glass hybrid outer skin, and a linear structural foam core infused with Pro-set epoxy resins.

SCUBA   an acronym for *self-contained underwater breathing apparatus*.

SD   the *secure digital* card offers the capability to record, store, review, and recall electronic data and displays on equipment designed for its use.

SE   an intercardinal direction, *South East*, or 135 degrees. It may be referenced either to Compass, Magnetic, or True North. *See also* Var

SE by E   *South East by East* is a compass direction. *SE by E* equals 123.75 degrees or 123 degrees 45 minutes. *See also* Var

SE by S *South East by South* is a compass direction. *SE by S* equals 146.25 degrees or 146 degrees 15 minutes. *See also* Var

S Fl an abbreviation used in NOAA charts to indicate a *short flashing light.*

sft *see so*

SH an abbreviation for the *ship's heading*. It is the direction a vessel points or heads at any given instant, expressed in angular degrees. The *heading* is constantly changing due to steering errors and the effects of the sea. The *heading* is also sometimes abbreviated as *Hdg. See* Hdg

Sh an italicized hydrographic abbreviation used in NOAA charts to indicate that the seabed at that point is *shells.*

SHA in celestial navigation the *sidereal hour angle* is the angle on the celestial sphere, measured westerly from *Aries* to another celestial body.

Shl an abbreviation used in NOAA charts to indicate a *shoal.*

Si an italicized hydrographic abbreviation used in NOAA charts to indicate that the seabed at that point is *silt.*

SIREN an abbreviation used in NOAA charts to indicate a *fog siren.*

S/M an italicized hydrographic abbreviation used in NOAA charts to indicate that the seabed at that point is *sand over mud.*

SMG   *speed made good* is the net speed from one point to another, disregarding any intermediate speed changes.

sml   an italicized hydrographic abbreviation used in NOAA charts to indicate *small*.

SMW   in IOR sail measurement rules this is the same as "G." *See* G; IOR

Sn   an italicized hydrographic abbreviation used in NOAA charts to indicate that the seabed at that point is *shingle*.

SNAME   the *Society of Naval Architects and Marine Engineers* is an international, non-profit, technical, professional society dedicated to advancing the art and science of naval architecture, ship building, and marine engineering.

so   an italicized qualifying term used on NOAA charts, meaning *soft*, and is used in conjunction with another hydrographic abbreviation. (i.e. *soM* means *soft mud*).

SOG   an abbreviation for *speed over ground*. It is the speed across the face of the earth, as opposed to the speed through the water.

SOLAS   an acronym for *safety of life at sea*, and establishes the minimum safety standards that have been agreed to by the *International Maritime Organization*. The SOLAS Convention, in its successive forms, is generally regarded as one of the most important of all international treaties concerning the safety of ships. The first version was adopted in 1914, in response to the *Titanic* disaster.

SONAR an acronym for *sound navigation and ranging*. It detects the location of underwater objects by means of sonic or supersonic waves reflected back from that object.

SORC the first of the *Southern Circuit* sailboat races was in 1941. Later it would be more formally known as the *Southern Ocean Racing Conference*. The series of five races included the St Petersburg-Havana Race, the Lipton Cup, the Miami-Nassau Race, the Governor's Cup in Nassau, and a race from Havana to Key West. Its popularity grew until 1973, before changes in offshore racing designs, and increasing demands on the leisure time of skippers and crews led to a waning interest in distance racing. The current popular format of an intense week of short circuit day-racing off Miami Beach made its debut in 1990 and the growth curve has turned upwards again.

SOS the first international distress radio signal was established in 1904 when *CQD* became the first Morse Code distress call. *CQ* was the call for all stations, and *D* was for distress. It was replaced in 1908 when *SOS* became the recognized distress call. When the *Titanic* sank is 1912, it sent out both *CQD* and *SOS*. *SOS* can be made by radio, light, or sound, and the pattern is three dots, three dashes, and three dots which, in Morse Code, translates to SOS: ■ ■ ■   ▬ ▬ ▬   ■ ■ ■   Some believe this was an abbreviation for *save our souls*.

Sp an abbreviation used in NOAA charts to indicate a *spire*.

SPDT a *single pole double throw* switch is an electrical switch that can select either of two circuits. *See also* SPST; SPDTCO; DPST; DPSTCO; DPDT; DPDTCO

Schematic Diagram for a
Single Pole Double Throw (SPDT) switch

SPDTCO a *single pole double throw center off* electrical switch is similar to a SPDT switch, but with a "center off" position. *See* SPDT

SPL in sail measurement, SPL is the *spinnaker pole length*, when the pole is fitted to the mast and set in a horizontal position athwartship, and measured from the centerline of the boat to the extreme outward end of the pole and fittings.

S'PIPE an abbreviation used in NOAA charts to indicate a *standpipe*.

SPOR the *shoreline plane of reference* is the high water datum level that defines and establishes the coastline.

SPST the *single pole single throw* electrical switch is a single-circuit on-off switch. *See also* SPDT; DPST; DPDT; SPDTCO; DPSTCO; DPDTCO

Schematic diagram for a
Single Pole Single Throw (SPST) switch

S/S or **S.S.** or **SS** this prefix is placed before the name of a ship to indicate that she is a merchant *steam ship*. Originally these letters stood for *screw steamship*, to differentiate it from paddle-wheelers.

SS   an abbreviation for *stainless steel*.

SSB   *single sideband* is a method of radio communication that reduces the necessary transmitter power and allows more stations to occupy a frequency band without interference. It is used by offshore vessels for long range communication in the medium and high frequency bands, and for ship-to-ship, ship-to Coast Guard, and e-mail.

SSCA   the *Seven Seas Cruising Association* was formed in 1952 and now has more than 10,000 members who share the dream of sailing the seas as a lifestyle. The association's monthly *Bulletin* gives practical cruising tips and accounts of members' voyages that help other members prepare for their own cruising adventures.

SSE   *South South East* is a compass direction. *SSE* equals 157.50 degrees or 157 degrees 30 minutes. *See also* Var

SSW   *South South West* is a compass direction. *SSW* equals 202.5 degrees or 202 degrees 30 minutes. *See also* Var

St   an italicized hydrographic abbreviation used in NOAA charts to indicate that the seabed at that point is *stones*.

Sta   the Coast Guard's abbreviation for *station*.

STBY   an abbreviation for *standby*.

STC   on a radar display the *sensitivity time control* is synonymous with "sea surface clutter suppression."

stk   *see sy*

St M or **St MI** an abbreviation for *statute mile*. The *statute mile* is 5,280 feet and is used as the reference for distances on some inland nautical charts.

STROBE an abbreviation for *stroboscope*. It is an intense, flashing light used for location purposes in emergency situations.

STV (antenna) a *satellite television antenna* system, which usually includes a satellite dish whose elevation and azimuth are electronically controlled to maintain satellite tracking as the boat rolls and pitches. This dish is usually enclosed within a protective dome.

Subm or **subm** an abbreviation used in NOAA charts to indicate *submerged*.

S/V the Coast Guard's abbreviation for *sailing vessel* or *sailboat*.

SVR gel batteries are *sealed valve-regulated* batteries that use pressure-release devices to keep the battery pressure at the optimum level.

SW an intercardinal direction, *South West*, or 225 degrees. See also Var

SW by S *South West by South* is a compass direction. SW by S equals 213.75 degrees or 213 degrees 45 minutes. See also Var

SW by W *South West by West* is a compass direction.. SW by W equals 236.25 degrees or 236 degrees 15 minutes. See also Var

SWR every transmission line (such as a coaxial cable) has its own *characteristic impedance*, which is determined by the physical characteristics of the transmission line, such as conductor size, spacing, and dielectric material. For maximum efficiency in transferring energy from a source (a transmitter) to a load (an antenna) the load's impedance must match that of the transmission line. If they don't match, part of the transmitted energy will be reflected back toward the source which adds or subtracts to the transmitted signal, creating *standing waves*. The ratio of the maximum to the minimum magnitude of the voltage or current of these *standing waves* is called the *standing wave ratio* (SWR). SWR meters are available that can be inserted into the transmission line and show the magnitude of *standing waves*. A high *SWR* could indicate an antenna or transmission line problem.

sy an italicized qualifying term used in conjunction with another hydrographic abbreviation on NOAA charts meaning *sticky*.

T

TANB the U.S. Coast Guard's *trailerable aids to navigation boats* are trailerable boats equipped with GPS monitors to accurately place or replace buoys and assist in other navigation tasks. *See also* ANT

TBT *tributylin tin* is a very effective bottom paint. However it has now been banned in many countries throughout the world due to its high and lasting toxicity to the marine environment. As of 2003 TBT has been outlawed in the U.S. for use on boats of under 82 feet in length.

TCPA   the *time to closest point of approach*. *See* CPA

TD   LORAN charts have overlays of the hyperbolic *time difference* lines of position created by a particular LORAN Group. By plotting the intersection of two or more of these TD lines, a fix can be determined. For LORANs that give latitude and longitude readouts, the intersection of these TDs are converted, through programmed algorithms, into a latitude and a longitude. *See* LORAN

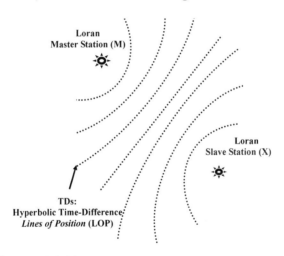

TDM   *see* TDMA

TDMA   an abbreviation for *time division multiple access*, a technology that delivers digital wireless service using *time division multiplexing* (TDM). TDMA is used by the GSM digital cellular system. *See also* CDMA; GSM

TDS Recon   this rugged, waterproof, lightweight, hand-held computer is made by Tripod Data Systems (TDS). It is being used in some Coast Guard districts as a new tool for faster satellite search and rescue operations.

(temp)   an enclosed abbreviation used in association with another term on NOAA charts to indicate that feature is *temporary*.

TFT   the *thin film transistor* display represents the cutting edge in flat-panel-display technology. It consists of transistors whose active current-carrying layer is a thin film. The TFT display can give better picture quality, contrast, and color, and is lighter, smaller, faster, and consumes less power than a LCD display but, at present, is much more expensive. *See* LCD

Tk   an abbreviation used in NOAA charts to indicate a *tank*.

TR   an abbreviation for *track*, the intended, anticipated, desired, or actual direction of movement across the face of the earth. *See also* CMG: COG

TR or **Tr**   an abbreviation used in NOAA charts to indicate a *tower*.

TRANSPAC   an acronym for the *Transpacific Yacht Race*, which starts in Los Angeles and ends in Hawaii.

TWCM   the *weather channel marine* is a satellite weather service delivery system for mobile services both on land and sea. It is in competition with XM WX, and the receiver and software system are provided on a monthly subscription basis. *See also* XM WX

TWD the *true wind direction* is the wind direction as perceived from a stationary position. See TWS

TWS the *true wind speed* is the speed and direction from which the wind is blowing as perceived from a stationary position. It is one of the vectors used in calculating the *apparent wind* on board a moving boat. See also AWA

U

UHF *ultra high frequency* is a range of frequencies in the electromagnetic spectrum, and includes frequencies from 328.6 megahertz (MHz) to 2.9 gigahertz (GHz). This UHF frequency band is sometimes generalized as 300 MHz to 3 GHz. See also Hz

UIN the *Unique Identifying Number*. See EPIRB.

UL *Underwriters Laboratories* is a world-wide certification organization that tests products and confirms their compliance with standards of public safety.

ULC the *Underwriters Laboratories of Canada*. See UL

ULDB an abbreviation for an *ultra light displacement boat*. These boats have long waterlines and narrow beams, with very light displacement. They flaunt traditional sailboat design and attract a different type of sailors—those for which performance means everything.

UPS   an *uninterruptible power supply* is a battery-operated system that is used to prevent or minimize voltage surges and spikes, voltage drops, total power failures, and frequency differences to sensitive electronic equipment. They come in two forms: the *standby UPS*, which only comes online when a problem is detected, and the *continuous UPS*, in which the equipment is constantly running off the UPS battery, which is constantly being recharged.

USCG   the abbreviation for the *United States Coast Guard*, the smallest of the seven uniformed services of the United States. It has a broad role in *Homeland Security*, law enforcement, search-and-rescue, marine environmental pollution response, and the maintenance of intracoastal and offshore aids to navigation. It was founded in 1790 as part of the *Department of the Treasury*, and in 1915 it became the *United States Coast Guard*, with the merger of the *National Lifesaving Service* and the *Revenue Cutter Service*. The *Coast Guard* later moved to the *Department of Transportation*, but in 2003 became part of the *Department of Homeland Security*.

USCGA   the *United States Coast Guard Auxiliary* was established by Congress in 1939 to assist the Coast Guard in promoting boating safety through educational programs, safety checks, safety patrols, search and rescue, and environmental protection. Its over 30,000 members come from all walks of life. *See also* USCG

USN   an abbreviation for the *United States Navy*, which was established in 1775, during the American Revolution, by General George Washington.

USPS   the *United States Power Squadrons* was organized in 1914 as a non-profit educational organization dedicated to making boating safer and more enjoyable by teaching classes in seamanship, navigation, and related subjects. There are about 60,000 members, organized into 450 squadrons across the country.

USS or **U.S.S.**   this prefix is placed before the name of a warship of the United States Navy and stands for *United States Ship*.

USYRU   the *United States Yacht Racing Union*, originally organized in 1897 as the *North American Yacht Racing Union* (NAYRU), was a private organization to promote yacht racing and provide racing and rating rules for the United States and Canada. In 1975 its name was changed to the USYRU, and its Canadian counterpart became the *Canadian Yachting Association* (CYA). Now, it receives its authority from an act of Congress. In 1991 its name was changed to the *United States Sailing Association*. *See also* CYA

UT   *Universal Time*. *See* UTC

UTB   the Coast Guard's abbreviation for *utility boat*.

UTC   *coordinated universal time* is based on the resonance of a Cesium-133 atom. The *National Institute of Standards and Technology Time and Frequency Division* broadcasts this atomic clock time from WWV and WWVB at Fort Collins, Colorado, and from WWVH in Kauai, Hawaii. *See also* WWV; WWVB; WWVH

UV an abbreviation for *ultra violet* radiation, whose wavelengths are just shorter than, and outside, the visible light spectrum. UV is emitted by our sun and other active objects in the cosmos, but most of this radiation is blocked by the ozone in our atmosphere.

V

V or **v** an abbreviation for volt(s), the unit of electrical potential difference.

v an italicized qualifying term used on NOAA charts, meaning *volcanic*, and is used in conjunction with another hydrographic abbreviation. (i.e *v*S).

Var *variation* is the difference, at any location, between the direction of the Earth's magnetic field and true north. This magnetic *variation* is shown on charts in a *compass rose*, which indicates whether the *variation* is to the east or west, the amount of that *variation*, and the expected annual change. The algebraic sum of *variation* and *deviation* is *compass error*. See also Dev; CE

VCG the *vertical center of gravity*. See Cg

VFO an abbreviation for *variable frequency oscillator*, which is needed in any radio transmitter or receiver that works on the superheterodyne principle, and which can be tuned to various frequencies.

VFO

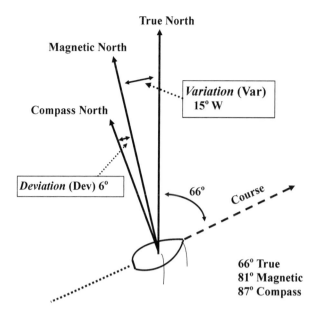

66° True
81° Magnetic
87° Compass

Showing the relationship of
***Deviation* (Dev) and *Variation* (Var)**

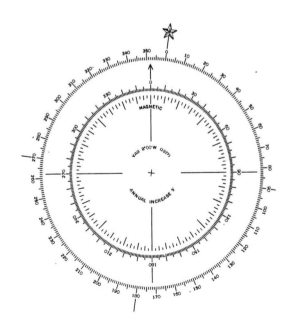

VGA the *video graphics array* is a graphics display system developed by IBM and used on PC and other display screens. It uses analog signals rather than digital signals.

VHF-FM this is the communications method of choice for the intracoastal and coastal recreational boater. VHF stands for *very high frequency*—the band of frequencies between 30 and 328.6 megahertz (MHz), with wavelengths of about 10 to 1 meter, respectively. The *marine band*, with frequencies between 156-163 MHz, is located within this broad vhf band. fm stands for *frequency modulation*. See also DSC; FM; MMSI

VIC *vessel information control* is a system, primarily used on large vessels, to monitor all of that vessel's operations.

VLF in the electromagnetic spectrum *very low frequencies* are those frequencies below 30 kHz. See also Hz

Vol see v

VOM an abbreviation for *volt/ohm meter*, the common hand-held multimeter with the capability of measuring AC and DC voltages, resistance (in ohms), and sometimes current (in amperes or milliamperes). See also ma

VPA *virtual population analysis* (or *cohort analysis*) is a technique used for the analysis of fished populations. The various VPA techniques show the estimated annual catches of a species for each year, the natural mortality rate, and the fishing mortality rate.

VQ or **V Qk Fl** an abbreviation used in NOAA charts to indicate a *very quick flashing light*

VRM on electronic navigational displays, VRM is an abbreviation for *variable range marker*. It is sometimes also called an EVRM, or *electronic variable range marker*.

W

W *West* is one of the cardinal directional points. It is 270 degrees, and may be referenced either to Compass, Magnetic, or True North. *See also* Var

WAAS the *wide area augmentation system* uses geostationary satellites, operating in the same frequency band as the GPS satellites, to provide corrections and reduce errors, resulting in increased accuracy for GPS receivers that are adapted and programmed to receive these WAAS signals. These potential GPS errors include clock errors; ionospheric and tropospheric delays as the signal travels from the satellites to Earth; Earth reflections; satellite orbital drifts; and control errors. The WAAS "stationary" satellites provide corrections that can be received directly on a WAAS GPS antenna, without the use of a separate low-frequency AM receiver and antenna such as is required with the *differential GPS* (DGPS) system. *See also* GPS; DGPS

W by N *West by North* is a compass direction. W by N equals 281.25 degrees or 281 degrees 15 minutes. *See also* Var

W by S *West by South* is a compass direction. W by S equals 258.75 degrees or 258 degrees 45 minutes. *See also* Var

Wd   an italicized hydrographic abbreviation used in NOAA charts to indicate that the seabed at that point is *weed* (including kelp).

WGS   the *world geodetic system* is a branch of geology that studies the shape of the Earth and determines the exact geographical points by defining the global reference frame for the Earth. With the advent of satellite mapping systems the accuracy of worldwide maps and charts have resulted in surveys that have become more accurate, culminating with the WGS-84 grid which, in the United States, is very similar to the NAD-83 model. WGS-84 is currently the reference system being used by the *global positioning system* (GPS). *See also* NAD

WGS-84   on current U.S. charts the horizontal reference *datum* is the *North American Datum of 1983* (NAD 83) which is considered to be the equivalent of the *World Geodetic System* 1984 (WGS 84). This is the default *datum* setting for most GPS receivers sold in the U.S. *See also* CD; NAD; NAD-83

wh   an italicized hydrographic abbreviation used in NOAA charts to indicate *white*.

WHIS   an abbreviation used in NOAA charts to indicate a *fog whistle*.

WHOI   the *Woods Hole Oceanographic Institute* is dedicated to research and higher education at the frontiers of ocean science. Its primary mission is to develop and effectively communicate a fundamental understanding of the processes and characteristics governing how the oceans function and how they interact with Earth as a whole.

WiFi an acronym for *wireless fidelity*. It is used in computer home networking and is a service available in many anchorages and marinas, allowing a boat's laptop to go online and have a wireless connection to the Internet. Most new laptops come with it built in, but on a boat, very often, higher power and an external antenna are necessary because of the distances involved.

Wk an abbreviation used in NOAA charts to indicate a *wreck*.

WL the *waterline* is the line where the surface of the water intersects the hull of a vessel. *See also* LWL; DL; WL

WMO the *World Meteorological Organization* is a specialized agency of the *United Nations*. It was established in 1950, and originated from the *International Meteorological Organization*. Its unique role in the *U.N.* facilitates the free exchange of data and information relating to meteorological events worldwide.

WNW *West North West* is a compass direction. *WNW* equals 292.5 degrees or 292 degrees 30 minutes. *See also* Var

WOT an abbreviation for *wide open throttle*—a term generally used when assessing boat performance. It refers to the top of an engine's rpm range.

WPL in sail measurement, "WPL" is the *whisker pole length*. It is the distance from the vertical center line of the forward face of the mast to the center of the clew cringle, or D-ring of the clew, of the jib to which the pole is attached, measured in a direction perpendicular to the vertical center line of the forward face of the mast.

WPR *World Powerboat Racing, Inc.* is a new organization founded in January 2005 by the combined resources of *Superboat International Productions, Inc* (SBIP), and the *American Powerboat Association* (ABPA) *Offshore Racing Association*. *See also* APBA; SBIP

WPT in electronic navigational gear a *waypoint* is a location or destination that is stored in the memory of that unit, and can be retrieved, displayed, and used for navigational purposes.

WS the *wetted surface* of a hull is the area of the submerged parts of the hull, including rudder and keel. A boat with a large *wetted surface* presents more friction with the water than a boat of small *wetted surface*.

WS an abbreviation, found more often in advertising copy for *wheel steering*.

WSI NOWrad this company provides access to weather radar via satellite, which is updated every five minutes. Weather reports, as well as current color radar images are available on a subscription basis. Animated images covering the previous two hours can also be displayed on the proprietary receiver.

WSW *West South West* is a compass direction. *WSW* equals 247.5 degrees or 247 degrees 30 minutes. *See also* Var

WWV WWV are the call-letters of one of the radio time-signal stations operated by the *National Institute of Science and Technology radio stations*. It started broadcasting time signals in 1923, and its current time signals are based on atomic clock technology with an accuracy of 1 part in 100 billion. The time signals are broadcast from Fort Collins, Colorado on frequencies of 2.5 MHz, 5.0 MHz, 10.0 MHz, 15.0 MHz, and 20.0 MHz. *See also* WWVB; WWVH

WWVB WWVB are the call letters of the radio station in Fort Collins, Colorado that broadcasts atomic-clock time signals on a frequency of 60 kHz. *See also* WWV; WWVH

WWVH WWVH are the call letters of the radio station in Kauai, Hawaii that broadcasts atomic clock time signals on 2.5 MHz, 5.0 MHz, 10.0 MHz, and 15.0 MHz. *See also* WWV; WWVB

Wx a common abbreviation for *weather*.

X

XMIT in electronic terminology "X" is a common abbreviation for "Trans," thus the abbreviation XMIT stands for *transmit*.

XM (radio) a company that provides satellite radio service on 150 digital channels. XM subscriptions run on a month-to-month basis.

XM WX a joint venture of XM Radio and Wx Works. It was established as a subscription service to display up-to-date weather reports on the screen associated with the XM WX receiver.

Y

YC the common abbreviation for *Yacht Club*.

yl an italicized hydrographic abbreviation used in NOAA charts to indicate *yellow*.

Z

Z in weather radar, Z is used to denote the reflected, return radar signal.

Zn this is the equivalent of *true azimuth*, and is the great-circle direction to any place from a given point. In celestial navigation it is used to designate the direction of a heavenly body.

ZT *zone time* was established to eliminate the confusion of multiple *local mean times* (LMT) in a given area. In *zone time*, all the places in a given zone, or band of longitudes, keep the same time, which is that of a specified meridian within the zone, usually the central meridian. *See also* LMT

PART II

EXCERPTS OF ABBREVIATIONS FROM NOAA'S *CHART NO. 1*

Charts, whether paper or electronic, are the most basic navigational necessity; but to interpret these charts it is necessary to understand the symbols and abbreviations used.

NOAA's *Chart No. 1—United States of America: Nautical Chart Symbols, Abbreviations, and Terms* is a publication that provides the symbology and abbreviations used on all U.S. charts, whether paper or electronic, as well as abbreviations used by the Coast Guard and other governmental agencies.

Appropriate sections of *Chart No. 1* (abbreviations that are of interest to recreational boaters) follow.

NOAA *Chart No.1*, Section "V"

Index of Abbreviations

AERO, Aero	Aero Light
Aero RC	Aeronautical radiobeacon
Al	Alternating
ALP	Articulating Loading Platform
Alt	Alternating
Am	Amber
anc	Ancient
ANCH, Anch	Anchorage
approx	Approximate
Apprs	Approaches
B	Bay, bayou
Bdy Mon	Boundary Monument
bk	Broken
Bkw	Breakwater
Bl	Blue
BM	Bench mark
Bn	Beacon
Bn Tr	Beacon tower
Br	Breakers
brg	Bearing
brk	Broken
Bu	Blue

c	Course
C	Can, cylindrical
C	Cove
CALM	Centenary Anchor Leg Mooring
Cas	Castle
Cb	Cobbles
cbl	Cable
cd	Candela
CD	Chart datum
Cem	Cemetery
CG	Coast Guard Station
Chan	Channel
Ch	Church
Chy	Chimney
Cl	Clay
CL	Clearance
cm	Centimeter(s)
Co	Coral
Co rf	Coral reef
Cr	Creek
crs	Course
Cup, Cup.	Cupola
Cus Ho	Customs house
Cy	Clay
D	Destroyed
Destr	Destroyed
dev	Deviation
DIA, Dio	Diaphone
Dir	Direction
dist	Distant
dm	Decimeter(s)
Dn	Dolphin
Dol	Dolphin

NOAA *Chart No. 1*, Section "V"

DW	Deep Water route
DZ	Danger Zone
E	East, eastern
ED	Existence doubtful
EEZ	Exclusive Economic Zone
E Int	Equal interval, isophase
Entr	Entrance
Est	Estuary
exper	Experimental
Explos	Explosive
Exting, exting	Extinguished
f	Fine
F	Fixed
Fd	Fjord
F Fl	Fixed and flashing
FISH	Fishing
Fl	Flashing
Fla	Flare stack
fm	Fathom
fms	Fathoms
fne	Fine
Fog Det Lt	Fog detector light
Fog Sig	Fog signal
FP	Flagpole
FS, FS.	Flagstaff
ft	Foot, feet
G	Gravel
G	Green
G	Gulf
Gp Fl	Group flashing
Gp Occ	Group occulting

h	Hard
h	Hour
H	Pilot transferred by helicopter
HAT	Highest astronomical tide
Hbr Mr	Harbormaster
Historic Wk	Historic Wreck
Hk	Hulk
Hor	Horizontally disposed
Hor Cl	Horizontal clearance
Hosp	Hospital
hr	Hour
hrd	Hard
IALA	International Association of Lighthouse Authorities
in	Inlet
Intens	Intensified
Int Qk Fl	Interrupted quick flashing
IQ	Interrupted quick flashing
I Qk Fl	Interrupted quick flashing
Iso	Isophase
IUQ	Interrupted ultra quick
km	Kilometer(s)
kn	Knot(s)
L	Loch, lough, lake
Lag	Lagoon
LANBY	Large Automatic Navigational Buoy
Lat, lat	Latitude
LASH	Lighter aboard ship
LAT	Lowest astronomical tide
Ldg	Landing
Ldg	Leading

Le	Ledge
L Fl	Long flashing
Lndg	Landing
LNG	Liquefied natural gas
Long, long	Longitude
LOP	Line of position
LPG	Liquefied petroleum gas
LSS	Life saving station
Lt	Light
Lt Ho	Lighthouse
Lt V	Light vessel
m	Meter(s)
m	Minute(s) of time
m	Medium (in relation to sand)
M	Mud, muddy
M	Nautical mile(s)
mag	Magnetic
MHHW	Mean higher high water
MHLW	Mean higher low water
MHW	Mean high water
MHWN	Mean high water neaps
MHWS	Mean high water springs
Mi	Nautical mile(s)
min	Minute of time
Mk	Mark
MLHW	Mean lower high water
MLLW	Mean lower low water
MLW	Mean low water
MLWN	Mean low water neaps
MLWS	Mean low water springs
mm	Millimeter(s)
Mo	Morse
MON, Mon	Monument
MSL	Mean sea level

Mt	Mountain
Mth	Mouth
N	North, northern
N	Nun
NE	Northeast
NM	Nautical mile(s)
N Mi	Nautical mile(s)
No	Number
Np	Neap tide
NW	Northwest
NWS SIG STA	Weather signal station
Obsc	Obscured
Obscd	Obscured
Obs spot	Observation spot
Obstn	Obstruction
Obstr	Obstruction
Oc	Occulting
Occ	Occulting
Occas	Occasional
ODAS	Ocean Data Acquisition System
Or	Orange
P	Pebbles
P	Pillar
PA	Position approximate
Pass	Passage
PD	Position doubtful
PLT STA	Pilot station
Pk	Peak
Post Off	Post office
Priv, priv	Private
Prod. Well	Production well

NOAA *Chart No. 1*, Section "V"

PROHIB	Prohibited
Pyl	Pylon
Q	Quick flashing
Qk Fl	Quick flashing
R	Coast radio station providing QTG services
R	Red
R	Rocky
Ra	Radar reference line
Ra (conspic)	Radar conspicuous object
Ra Antenna	Dish aerial
Racon	Radar transponder beacon
Radar Sc.	Radar scanner
Radar Tr.	Radar tower
Radome, Ra Dome	Radar dome
Ra Ref	Radar reflector
RBn	Circular radiobeacon
RC	Circular radiobeacon
Rd	Roads, roadstead
RD	Directional radiobeacon
RDF	Radio direction finding station
Ref.	Refuge
Rep	Reported
Rf	Reef
RG	Radio direction finding station
Rk	Rock
Rky	Rocky
R Mast	Radio mast
Ro Ro	Roll on Roll off
R Sta	Coast radio station providing QTG services
R Tower	Radio tower

Ru	Ruins
Rw	Rotating radiobeacon
S	Sand
S	South, southern
S	Spar, spindle
s	Second of time
SALM	Single Anchor Leg Mooring
SBM	Single Buoy Mooring
Sc	Scanner
Sd	Sound
SD	Sounding doubtful
SE	Southeast
sec	Second of time
sf	Stiff
sft	Soft
Sh	Shells
Shl	Shoal
Si	Silt
so	Soft
Sp	Spring tide
SP	Spherical
Sp.	Spire
Spipe	Standpipe
SPM	Single point mooring
SS	Signal station
st	Stones
stf	Stiff
stk	Sticky
Str	Strait
Subm	Submerged
Subm pipes	Submerged pipes
sy	Sticky
SW	Southwest

T	True
t	Metric ton(s)
Tel	Telephone, telegraph
Temp, temp	Temporary
Tk	Tank
Tr, Tr., TR	Tower
TT	Tree tops
TV Mast	Television mast
TV Tower	Television tower
Uncov	Uncovers
UQ	Ultra quick
v	Volcanic
var	Variation
Vert	Vertically disposed
Vert Cl	Vertical clearance
Vi	Violet
Vil	Village
VLCC	Very large crude carrier
vol	Volcanic
VQ	Very quick
V Qk Fl	Very quick flash
W	West, western
W	White
Wd	Weed
WGS	World Geodetic System
Whf	Wharf
WHIS, Whis	Whistle
Wk	Wreck
Y	Yellow

NOAA *Chart No. 1*, Section "V"

Index of Abbreviations:
Supplementary National Abbreviations

Apt	Apartment
B	Black
bk	Black
bl	Black
Blds	Boulders
br	Brown
bu	Blue
Cap	Capitol
ch	Chocolate
Chec	Checkered
Ck	Chalk
Cn	Cinders
Co	Company
Co Hd	Coral head
COL REGS	Collision regulations
Corp	Corporation
Cps	Cycles per second
CRD	Columbia River Datum
c/s	Cycles per second
Ct Ho	Court house

dec	Decayed
deg	Degree(s)
Di	Diatoms
Diag	Diagonal bands
Discol water	Discolored water
dk	Dark
Explos Anch	Explosives anchorage
Facty	Factory
F Gp Fl	Fixed and group flashing
fl	Flood
fly	Flinty
Fr	Foraminifera
Fu	Fucus
GAB, Gab	Gable
GCLWD	Gulf Coast Low Water Datum
Gl	Glabigerina
glac	Glacial
gn	Green
Govt Ho	Government house
Grd	Ground
Grs	Gross
gty	Gritty
GUN	Fog gun
gy	Gray
HECP	Harbor entrance control point
HHW	Higher high water
HS	High school
ht	Height
HW	High water
HWF & C	High water full and change

Hz	Hertz
in	Inch
ins	Inches
Inst	Institute
ISLW	Indian springs low water
K	Kelp
kc	Kilocycle
kHz	Kilohertz
kn	Knot(s)
La	Lava
LLW	Lower low water
LOOK TR	Lookout tower
lrg	Large
lt	Light
Ltd	Limited
LW	Low water
LWD	Low water datum
LWF & C	Low water full and change
m^2	Square meter(s)
m^3	Cubic meter(s)
Ma	Mattes
Magz	Magazine
Mc	Megacycle(s)
Mds	Modrepores
MHz	Megahertz
Ml	Marl
Mn	Manganese
Mo	Morse code
Ms	Mussels
MTL	Mean tide level

NAUTO	Nautophone
or	Orange
Oys	Oysters
Oz	Ooze
Pav	Pavilion
Pm	Pumice
Po	Polyzoa
Pt	Pteropods
Q	Quarantine
Qz	Quartz
Rd	Radiolaria
rd	Red
rt	Rotten
Ry	Railway, railroad
Sc	Scariae
Sch	Schist
Sch	School
Sem	Semaphore
Sh	Shingle
S-LFl	Short-long flashing
sml	Small
Spg	Sponge
Spi	Spicules
spk	Speckled
Stg	Seatangle
St M	Statute mile(s)
St Mi	Statute mile(s)
Str	Stream
str	Streaky

NOAA *Chart No. 1*, Section "V"

SUB-BELL	Submarine fog bell
Subm crib	Submerged crib
SUB-OSC	Submarine oscillator
Sub vol	Submarine volcano
T	Telephone
T	Short ton(s)
T	Tufa
Tel	Telegraph
Tel off	Telegraph office
ten	Tenacious
unev	Uneven
Univ	University
µs	Microsecond(s)
µsec	Microsecond(s)
vard	Varied
vel	Velocity
vi	Violet
Vol Ash	Volcanic ash
wh	White
WHIS	Whistle
yd	Yard
yds	Yards
yl	Yellow

NOAA *Chart No 1*, Section "W"

International Abbreviations

Positions, Distances, Directions, Compass

PA	Position approximate
PD	Position doubtful
N	North
E	East
S	South
W	West
NE	Northeast
SE	Southeast
NW	Northwest
SW	Southwest
km	Kilometer(s)
m	Meter(s)
dm	Decimeter(s)
cm	Centimeter(s)
mm	Millimeter(s)
M	Nautical mile(s), Sea mile(s)
ft	Foot, feet
h	Hour
m, min	Minute(s) of time
s, sec	Second(s) of time
kn	Knot(s)

t	ton(s)
cd	Candela (new candela)

Cultural Features

Ru	Ruin

Ports

Lndg	Landing for boats
RoRo	Roll-on, Roll-off ferry

Depths

ED	Existence doubtful
SD	Sounding doubtful

Rocks, Wrecks, Obstructions

Br	Breakers
Wk	Wreck
Obstn	Obstruction

Offshore Installations, Submarine Cables, Submarine Pipelines

Fla	Flare stack
Prod	Submerged Production
Well	Well

Tracks, Routes

Ra	Radar
DW	Deep Water

NOAA *Chart No. 1*, Section "W"

Areas, Limits

No	Number
DW	Deep Water

Hydrographic Terms

SMt	Seamount

Lights

Lt	Light
F	Fixed
Oc	Occulting
Iso	Isophase
Fl	Flashing
LFl	Long-flashing
Q	Quick
IQ	Interrupted quick
VQ	Very quick
IVQ	Interrupted very quick
UQ	Ultra quick
IUQ	Interrupted ultra quick
Mo	Morse
W	White
R	Red
G	Green
Bu	Blue
Vi	Violet
Y	yellow/orange/Amber
Or	orange
Am	Amber
Ldg	Leading light
Dir	Direction light

occas	occasional
R Lts	Air obstruction lights
Fog Det Lt	Fog detector light
Aero	Aeronautical

Buoys, Beacons

B	Black
Mk	Mark
IALA	International Association of Lighthouse Authorities

Fog Signals

Explos	Explosive
Dia	Diaphone
Whis	Whistle

Radar, Radio, Electronic Position-Fixing Systems

Ra	Coast Radar Station
Racon	Radar transponder beacon
RC	Circular (non-directional) marine radiobeacon
RD	Directional radiobeacon
RW	Rotating-pattern radiobeacon
RG	Radio direction-finding stations
R	QTG service, Coast radio stations
Aero RC	Aeronautical radiobeacon
WGS	World Geodetic System

NOAA *Chart No. 1*, Section "W"

Services

H	Pilots transferred by helicopter
SS	Signal station
INT	International

Other books of interest from Sheridan House:

MAINSAIL TO THE WIND
A Book of Sailing Quotations
by William Galvani

Throughout history, the sea and those who sail upon it have frequently been the subjects of literature, poetry, speeches, songs, and adages. Now, for the first time, the best of these musings have been collected in a single volume. **Mainsail to the Wind** presents over 1,000 quotes from writers and speakers around the world, conveniently organized into 70 categories for browsing and indexed by keywords and author for easy reference.
"The author has gathered the best and most memorable . . . in this book."—*Latitudes & Attitudes*

WITH A PINCH OF SALT
A Collection of Nautical Expressions and Other Stories
by Captain Nick Bates

"A delightful collection of stories explaining the origins of so many well-known nautical sayings and expressions told in a humoristic way and illustrated with clever cartoons. A must for anybody who professes to know anything about sea and ships."—*White Ensign Association*

ADVICE TO THE SEALORN
by Herb Payson

". . . covers a broad range of cruising topics in an informative and entertaining manner. Whether planning to extend your cruise or live aboard, this is good reading."—*Cruising World*

SOMETHING BORROWED
by Joel Graffley

"With hundreds of innovative improvements described, it's a useful book for those who love tinkering aboard their boats—and who also love gadgets!"—*Sailing Inland & Offshore*
"The handiest sailing tips book ever . . . full of gems that will keep any cruising sailor busy."—*Sailing*

SHERIDAN HOUSE
America's Favorite Sailing Books
www.sheridanhouse.com

Other books of interest from Sheridan House:

SAILING LANGUAGE
by Elliot Dunlap Smith and Thomas R. Moore

Like all human endeavors, sailing has its own unique language,
a rich terminology reflecting the ancient origin
and sophisticated nature of the sport.

". . . a serious attempt to lay out and define the words used to talk about sailing in all its forms, to allow a novice to speak to the old tars with confidence and, above all, correctly."—*The Ellsworth American*

THE PERFECT FIRST MATE
A Woman's Guide to Recreational Boating
by Joy Smith

"Well written, humorous, and full of useful info for the experienced as well as the novice."—*Latitudes & Attitudes*

". . . a helpful collection of tips to make any outing more enjoyable, whether it's a day trip or an extended cruise."—*Boating World*

". . . the knowledge contained in this book will make your boating experiences much more pleasurable."—*THE ENSIGN*

THINGS I WISH I'D KNOWN BEFORE I STARTED SAILING
by John Vigor

There are many frustrated sailors out there and with the baby boomers starting to retire many finally have the freedom to indulge their sailing dreams. This book is intended to guide them. Aimed at sailboat owners of all kinds, this reference book contains 200 entries packed with solid practical advice and valuable tips.

"This is a great reference book for those just entering the world of sailing, and entertaining 'Ah yes' for seasoned sailors who will identify and agree with the author's findings."—*Latitudes & Attitudes*

A MARINER'S MISCELLANY
by Peter H. Spectre

"If you weren't already infected by the call of the sea, this book will do the trick."—*SAIL* Magazine

"From tall ship lore to small boat savvy, from grog recipes to rowing terms and techniques, Spectre has collected a vast store of knowledge and recounted it in a most enjoyable fashion. It's a book one can open to any page and find something that will educate, entertain, and motivate."—*Sea History*

SHERIDAN HOUSE
America's Favorite Sailing Books
www.sheridanhouse.com

Other books of interest from Sheridan House:

A•B•SEA
A Loose-footed Lexicon
by Jack Lagan

". . . an enjoyably eclectic mix of clear factual definitions of today's everyday boating terms with more arcane expressions and curious digressions by the author . . . Highly recommended."—*Watercraft*

". . . [An] entertaining dictionary of the language and legends of seafarers of the 21st century."—*Research and Reference Book News*

CREATIVE ROPECRAFT
by Stuart Grainger

". . . the best book about ropes and knots that I have read. . . . You'll be amazed at what you can accomplish just by following the instructions in Creative Ropecraft."—*THE ENSIGN*

"The best fancy knotting book in recent times . . . only when you've tried can you know just how good."—*Knotting Matters*

". . . an excellent handbook on standard and decorative knot work; first-class, easy-to-follow step-by-step diagrams."—*WoodenBoat*

THE RUDDER TREASURY
A Companion for Lovers of Small Craft
Edited by Tom Davin

". . . quite simply the most engaging fall-cruising reading any skipper could stow in his ship's library. Stoke the stove, lean back on the settee, and savor the wisdom and genius."—*Cruising World*

". . . a treasure of good writing, good humor and good advice."—*Points East*

COMMUNICATION AT SEA
Marine Radio, Email, Satellite and Internet Services
by Mike Harris

"There are procedures, protocols and codes. It all forms a nice wrap-up of current communications technologies."—*Sailing & Yachting, (S/*

". . . will help you cut through the sales hype and see what systems really work for the cruising sailor."—*Latitude & Attitudes*

SHERIDAN HOUSE
America's Favorite Sailing
www.sheridanhouse.